Building A Better Data Warehouse

Don Meyer
and Casey Cannon

Foreword by
David V. Gelardi

To join a Prentice Hall PTR Internet mailing list, point to
http://www.prenhall.com/mail_lists/

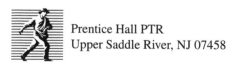

Prentice Hall PTR
Upper Saddle River, NJ 07458

ISBN 0-13-890757-9

9 780138 907570

90000

Library of Congress Cataloging-in-Publication Data

Meyer, Don
  Building a better data warehouse / by Don Meyer and Casey Cannon.
      p.   cm.
  Includes index
    ISBN 0-13-890757-9
    1. Data warehousing. I. Cannon, Casey. II. Title.
  QA76.9.D37M49 1998
  005.75'6--dc21   97-38980
                                     CIP

Editorial/Production Supervision: *Eileen Clark*
Acquisitions Editor: *Gregory G. Doench*
Marketing Manager: *Stephen Solomon*
Buyer: *Alexis R. Heydt*
Cover Design: *Design Source*
Cover Design Direction: *Jerry Votta*
Editorial Assistant: *Mary Treacy*

© 1998 Prentice Hall PTR
Prentice-Hall, Inc.
A Simon & Schuster Company
Upper Saddle River, NJ 07458

Prentice Hall books are widely used by corporations and government agencies for training, marketing, and resale. The publisher offers discounts on this book when ordered in bulk quantities.

For more information, contact
        Corporate Sales Department,
        Phone: 800-382-3419; FAX: 201-236-7141
        E-mail (Internet): corpsales@prenhall.com
Or write: Prentice Hall PTR
        Corp. Sales Department
        One Lake Street
        Upper Saddle River, NJ 07458

Printed in the United States of America

10 9 8 7 6 5 4 3 2 1

ISBN 0-13-890757-9

Prentice-Hall International (UK) Limited, *London*
Prentice-Hall of Australia Pty. Limited, *Sydney*
Prentice-Hall Canada Inc., *Toronto*
Prentice-Hall Hispanoamericana, S.A., *Mexico*
Prentice-Hall of India Private Limited, *New Delhi*
Prentice-Hall of Japan, Inc., *Tokyo*
Simon & Schuster Asia Pte. Ltd., *Singapore*
Editora Prentice-Hall do Brasil, Ltda., *Rio de Janeiro*

To Granddaddy
—*Casey*

To My Family
—*Don*

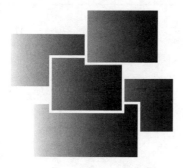

TABLE OF CONTENTS

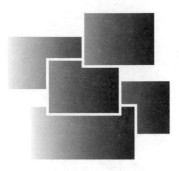

PREFACE

The *data warehouse* enables users to access vast stores of integrated, operational data to track business trends, facilitate forecasting and planning efforts, and make strategic decisions. It is not a single product, but rather a flexible environment comprised of multiple technologies. It consolidates operational data from all departments within an organization into a relational database and molds the data into a subject-oriented format that is easy for end-users to access and analyze. The most significant trend to emerge from information technology in the 1990s, data warehousing puts the information technology organization in a position to significantly improve its company's competitiveness.

The data warehouse market is hot. And, it's getting hotter. The past few years have seen explosive growth, both in the number of products and services offered and in the adoption of these technologies by corporations. Consider the following excerpt from an article by Ken Rudin, "What's New in Data Warehousing," *DBMS*, v9, Aug., 1996 p4(5):

> *A February, 1996 survey by the META Group (Stamford, Conn.) found that 95 percent of companies surveyed intend to build a data warehouse. Granted, many of these companies have unique ideas about what constitutes a data warehouse, but what's most interesting is that in 1994, that number was only 15 percent.*
>
> *Various estimates (including those of the META Group) put the size of the data warehouse market (which includes all hardware, database software, and*

access tools) at $2 billion. This number will grow to $8 billion by 1998, which translates into a 60 percent average annual growth rate. Additionally, this $8 billion will be complemented by another $5 billion in integration services.

Not only is the market growing, but individual data warehouse applications are also growing. Again drawing on the recent META Group survey, 60 percent of those surveyed expected their data warehouses to grow beyond 50GB by mid 1996, and at the same time they will need to support more than 50 users.

Still, those pondering building a data warehouse should exercise a healthy dose of caution-less than 15 percent are currently in full production. There are many reasons for this. One reason is simply that the exponential growth rate of new data warehouse projects implies that the majority of these projects have only recently started. However, another set of reasons is a little more troubling. Corporations are learning that large data warehouse projects cost more dollars and take more time than originally thought. On average, when implementing a data warehouse project, corporations spend $2 million on hardware and $1 million on software and services, and the project takes 12 to 18 months.

Is your company building a data warehouse or considering building a data warehouse? Data warehousing is quickly coming into the mainstream of information technology. It's impossible to pick up a trade publication or an industry analysis without reading something about data warehousing. The reports and surveys coming from many of the leading analysts show that the majority of information technology organizations are implementing a data warehouse.

Every technology company has re-positioned products or services to be data warehousing products or services, hoping to cash in on the data warehousing boom. Both implementors of data warehousing technology and the companies who sell the technology, corresponding services, and support see data warehousing as a gold mine. Industries hope that data warehousing will unearth previously unexploited markets within their data, enabling them to make more informed decisions on product design, pricing, and marketing. Warehouse technologists see the rush to build data warehouses and are counting on warehouse product and service sales. Chances are, both groups will benefit. Gartner Group's *Data Warehouses: Clarifying the Hype & Confusion*, January 22, 1997, places the data warehouse market size at $6 billion. And, companies rolling out advanced data warehouse systems are enabling multiple functions outside marketing to share information and allocate enterprise resources to optimize long-term profitable customer relationships.

How To Use This Book

This book provides the members of a data warehouse implementation team with the information (and specific steps) they need to build a data warehouse. Data warehouse books have typically had plenty of conceptual and academic data, but have been pretty light on specifics—primarily due to the newness of the market. Now that every vendor and consulting company has repositioned products and services to be data warehousing products and services, this book will enable you to understand what really comprises a data warehouse, understand who will be doing what to build the warehouse, and identify the tools each team member will need.

Building a Better Data Warehouse is structured around a data warehouse implementation methodology. We've designed this book sequentially, providing a foundation in Section 1 and then moving to design and implementation in Sections 2 and 3. Designing, building, and deploying a data warehouse usually involves multiple groups, including executives, business analysts, end-users, technical staff, and support staff. Each chapter corresponds to specific team member's responsibilities, reviewing expectations, requirements, implementation specifics, and providing example deliverables. (Note that each chapter is similar to the data warehouse seminars you've been attending or have been thinking about attending; for example, Data Warehousing for DBAs, Data Warehousing for Data Modelers, Data Warehousing General Overview for Executives.) [1]

Section 1, Introducing the Data Warehouse, introduces executives and managers *to* data warehousing while briefing them on what to expect while building and then deploying the data warehouse. We then dive into data warehousing terms, concepts, frameworks, and components to enable project managers, business analysts, information technology staff, and end-users to talk the same language while making the decisions necessary to build the data warehouse.

Section 2, Managing the Data Warehouse Construction, is targeted at the project manager and initial data warehouse team, which are focused on building the project scope document and project plan deliverables while gathering end-user requirements. Section 2 walks designers, developers, and administrators through hardware platforms and operating systems, databases, tools, and application comparisons, identifying the key vendors and products. This is not an all-encompassing guide to every vendor's product line, but rather a strengths and weaknesses assessment of products in the data warehousing space.

---

1. A glossary of abbreviations and acronyms is included at the end of this book.

Section 3, **Building the Data Warehouse**, is primarily targeted at the data modeler and DBA—along with other members of the data warehouse construction team. We focus on the steps required to complete the data model deliverables, as well as the steps required by the DBA to undertake the physical construction of the data warehouse. Discussions of meta data, extraction programming, populating the data warehouse, end-user access tools, and training are found in Section 3.

For those reading closely, you might notice a bit of information overlap. We introduce the ideas and concepts of data warehousing in Section 1 and then follow up with applicable tools, development, and deployment issues in Sections 2 and 3.

Summary

So, why should you take our word for any of this? Well, we can help you learn from our mistakes—*Building a Better Data Warehouse* reflects our hands-on experience with data warehousing. Want a quick synopsis of our mistakes? Well, for starters, don't let anyone talk you out of... paying attention to data integrity; thinking about scalability; sticking to the open systems standard, UNIX; choosing vendors with a proven track record; undertaking a pilot project; and, training users in the new tools. (Oh, and there's more! We'll confess to additional snafus throughout the book.)

Don Meyer is president of Don Meyer & Associates, Inc. He advises clients on all aspects of database administration, UNIX/network administration, and client/server and data warehouse implementation, including conducting training courses and database performance audits. His data warehouse clients have included MCI, Southland, CompuAdd, and Citicorp. Don is Oracle 7 DBA certified and has published articles on client/server and data warehousing.

Casey Cannon is a member of IBM's RS/6000 Division technical staff and is the co-author of *PowerPC: Concepts, Architecture and Design* (McGraw Hill), as well as *Simply AIX* (Prentice Hall). She has been part of RS/6000 development and strategy for the past five years and is currently part of the RS/6000 team focusing on electronic commerce, collaboration, content, and Internet Service Providers in the network computing space.

Want help designing, building, and deploying your data warehouse? Or, are things not going quite as you originally envisioned? We discuss the following vendors and consultants throughout this book; give them a call for advice, help, and/or product information.

Andyne Computing	(613) 548-4355
Arbor Software	(800) 858-1666
Brio Technology	(415) 856-8000
Cognos	(800) 4-Cognos
Compaq	(800) OK-Compaq
Computer Associates	www.cai.com
Data Warehousing Institute	www.dw-institute.com
DataMind	(415) 364-5580
Datawatch	(508) 988-9700
DBMX	(415) 778-8350
Don Meyer & Associates, Inc.	donmeyer@mindspring.com
Hewlett-Packard	(800) 752-0900
IBM	(800) IBM-2468
Information Advantage	(800) 959-OLAP
Information Builders	(800) 969-INFO
Informix	(800) 331-1763
Intelligent Solutions, Inc.	www.intelsols.com
Intersolv	(800) 547-4000
Lotus Development	(800) 343-5414
Microsoft	(800) 426-9400
MicroStrategy	(703) 848-8600
NCR	www.ncr.com
Oracle	(800) 633-0596
Pilot Software	(800) 944-0094
PLATINUM Technology	(800) 442-6861
Prism	(408) 752-1888
Red Brick	(800) 777-2585
Software AG	www.sagus.com
Sun Microsystems	www.sun.com
Sterling Software	(800) 522-4252
Sybase	(800) 792-2731

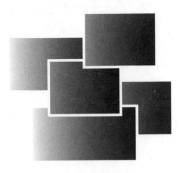

FOREWORD

Why a Data Warehouse? is fast becoming a rhetorical question. It is recognized that investing in the technologies, skills, and methodologies that IBM has termed Business Intelligence is key to extending a company's competitive advantage. Our investigations indicate that the applications companies most often deploy focus on one of two categories. The first category focuses on internal levers—for example, buying power or pricing or promotional effectiveness. The second focuses on customers—Who are they? What are their buying habits? How do I know them (to increase their satisfaction with my services or products)? This application focus in conjunction with the falling cost of storage, servers, and software as well as the rapid innovation in analytic and visualization techniques and, dare I say it, Data Mining, has enabled many, many customers to be extremely successful in achieving huge competitive gains with careful and deliberate Business Intelligence application deployments.

Today, the question most asked by customers has shifted away from why to how. This book, *Building a Better Data Warehouse*, provides answers to this seemingly simple but oh-so-fascinating question. The number of decisions and approaches that can be deployed on the path to actionable information is mind boggling. As explained in this book, a deliberate and programmatic approach to extending the information access architecture across the enterprise enables a company to achieve its goals with a minimum time investment while maximizing inter- and intra-enterprise data access flexibility.

IBM is uniquely positioned to be a major partner in this task of 1) architecting and constructing the Data Warehouse; and 2) deploying the downstream applications (frequently the reason for building the warehouse in the first place). We have a variety of hardware platforms from each of our server groups—AS/400, S/390, the PC Company, and the RS/6000 (with the industry leading RS/6000 SP). Our software business, built on the DB2 product family, can provide much of the necessary infrastructure to build, manage and feed the corporate repository that the warehouse is. Our award-winning data mining software, Intelligent Miner and its associated Business Discovery Solutions applications, provide a powerful base for ferreting out the complex but critical patterns and relationships that enable more effectiveness in business processes. Our storage products manage the large amount of data that Business Intelligence applications demand. We have invested in and developed specialized consulting skills and services for the deployment of industry-specific data models and context sensitive applications. And, we have forged alliances with a variety of partners bringing their software products and point-specific skills to the table while absorbing much of the risk of you being your own general contractor.

In a very real sense, building a Business Intelligence solution is analogous to constructing a building. Consider using this book as a resource guide for that complex construction task. It is certainly not a theoretical treatise that explores the various methods and technologies that could be used for this job. Rather it is a pragmatic instruction manual that guides an organization through the step-by-step task of creating this "building." The basis of the prescribed approach is the successful and hands-on implementation of data warehouse projects—let this book help you avoid the pitfalls that many have encountered on their journeys to a new decision process.

In thinking about the many, many customers that I have had the pleasure of working with as they have struggled though the evaluation of technologies and then begun an implementation plan, I am struck by how valuable it would have been to have left this textbook behind. I cannot stress enough the value of discipline and focus in these projects. Our marketing messages have evolved over time to a simple but powerful statement that is underlined by this book and could have saved countless hours of indirection and wasted energy, Think Big, Act Small. Think and plan for a large enterprise warehouse but act on a very small set of real business problems. Let that one or two problems drive the process while working towards the creation and deployment of the Enterprise Data Warehouse. Use your business intelligence to extend your competitive advantage.

—David Gelardi
IBM Program Director for Business
Intelligence & DBMS Marketing
for the RS/6000 Division

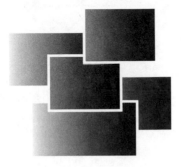

ACKNOWLEDGMENTS

We would like to thank Donald B. Meyer for his time and energy in creating the caricatures for each chapter, as well as David V. Gelardi, IBM's Program Director for Business Intelligence and DBMS Marketing for the RS/6000 Division, for writing the Foreword.

TRADEMARKS

Adobe is a trademark of Adobe Systems Incorporated
ADABAS and NATURAL are trademarks of SOFTWARE AG
AdStar is a trademark of International Business Machines Corporation
AIX is a trademark of International Business Machines Corporation
AIX/6000 is a trademark of International Business Machines Corporation
Arbor and Essbase are trademarks of Arbor Software Corporation
AS/400 is a trademark of International Business Machines Corporation
Brio, Brio.Insight, and BrioQuery are trademarks of Brio Technology, Inc.
Business Objects is a trademark of Business Objects, Inc.
CA-OpenIngres is a trademark of Computer Associates International, Inc.
CICS is a trademark of International Business Machines Corporation
Cognos, Impromptu, and PowerPlay are trademarks of Cognos, Inc.
Crystal Reports and Holos are trademarks of Seagate Technology, Inc.
DataGuide and DB2 Extenders are trademarks of International Business Machines Corporation
DataJoiner is a trademark of International Business Machines Corporation
Data Propagator is a trademark of International Business Machines Corporation
DB2 is a trademark of International Business Machines Corporation
DB2/6000 is a trademark of International Business Machines Corporation
Data Interpretation System is a trademark of International Business Machines Corporation
DecisionSuite, DecisionSuite Server, and WebOLAP are trademarks of Information Advantage, Inc.
Developer/2000, Designer/2000, Database Server, Oracle CASE, Oracle Data Browser, Oracle Data Query,
  Oracle Workgroup Server [or Oracle 7 Workgroup Server], Oracle 7, and Oracle 8 are trademarks of
  Oracle Corporation
Distributed Computing Environment (DCE) is a trademark of Open Software Foundation, Inc.
Distributed Relational Database Architecture is a trademark of International Business Machines Corporation
DEC is a trademark of Digital Equipment Corporation
DSS Server is a trademark of MicroStrategy, Inc.
Enterprise Data Access/SQL and EDA/SQL are trademarks of Information Builders, Inc.
ERwin, ERwin/ERX, and ERwin/OPEN are trademarks of Logic Works, Inc.

Esperant and NATURAL LightStorm are trademarks of Software AG, Inc.

Evolutionary Technologies International and ETI EXTRACT are trademarks of Evolutionary Technologies International, Inc.

HP, and HP Intelligent Warehouse are trademarks of Hewlett-Packard Company

HP-US is a trademark of Hewlett-Packard Company

IA Decision Support Suite is a trademark of Information Advantage, Inc.

IBM is a trademark of International Business Machines Corporation

Informatica, Informatica Design, and PowerMart are trademarks of Informatica Corporation

Information Warehouse is a trademark of International Business Machines Corporation

Informix, INFORMIX-Universal Server, INFORMIX-OnLine Extended Parallel Server, INFORMIX-OnLine Dynamic Server, INFORMIX-MetaCube, INFORMIX-OnLine Workgroup Server, and INFORMIX-OnLine Workstation, DataBlade and INFORMIX-MetaCube are trademarks of Informix Software, Inc.

IQ/Vision is a trademark of IQ Software Corporation, Inc.

Intel is a trademark of Intel Corporation

IPX and Netware is a trademark of Novell Corporation, Inc.

IPX/SPX is a trademark of Ideographics, Inc.

Key:Plan is a trademark of Sterling Software

Lotus and Lotus 1-2-3 is a trademark of Lotus Development Corporation

Lotus Notes is a trademark of Lotus Development Corporation

Microsoft, Excel, VisualBasic, Windows, Windows NT, MSN, and SQL Server are trademarks of Microsoft Corporation

Oracle and Oracle Express Analyzer is a trademark of Oracle Corporation

PASSPORT is a trademark of Carleton Corporation, Inc.

Patrol is a trademark of BMC Software, Inc.

Pentium is a trademark of Intel Corporation

Pilot Analysis Server and Pilot Desktop are trademarks of Pilot Software, Inc.

PLATINUM Data Shopper is a registered trademark of Platinum Technology, Inc.

PLATINUM InfoPump is a registered trademark of Platinum Technology, Inc.

PLATINUM Repository is a registered trademark of Platinum Technology, Inc.

PLATINUM Forest & Trees, PLATINUM InfoTransport, and PLATINUM Repository are trademarks of Platinum Technology, Inc.

POWER Architecture is a trademark of International Business Machines Corporation

PowerBuilder is a trademark of Powersoft Business Group of Sybase, Inc.

PowerPC is a trademark of International Business Machines Corporation

POWERstation is a trademark of International Business Machines Corporation

Prism Directory Manager is a trademark of Prism Solutions, Inc.

Prism Solutions, Inc. is a trademark of Prism Solutions, Inc.

Prism Warehouse Directory and Prism Warehouse Manager are trademarks of Prism Solutions, Inc.

Rational Rose is a trademark of Rational Software Corporation

Red Brick is a registered trademark of Red Brick Systems

Red Brick Warehouse is a trademark of Red Brick Systems

ReportSmith is a trademark of Borland International, Inc.

RS/6000 is a trademark of International Business Machines Corporation

RS/6000 SP is a trademark of International Business Machines Corporation

SAS System is a trademark of SAS Institute, Inc.

SILVERRUN-Professional Suite, SILVERRUN-Entity Relationship eXpert, SILVERRUN-Relational Data modeler, SILVERRUN-Business Process Modeler, and SILVERRUN-Workgroup Repository Manager are trademarks of SILVERRUN Technologies, Inc.

Solaris is a trademark of Sun Microsystems, Inc.

SPARCstation is a trademark of Sun Microsystems, Inc.

SQL Server is a trademark of Microsoft Corporation

Sun is a trademark of Sun Microsystems, Inc.

SYBASE is a registered trademark of Sybase, Inc.

SYBASE IQ is a registered trademark of Sybase, Inc.
SYBASE SQL Server is a registered trademark of Sybase, Inc.
System Architect is a trademark of Popkin Software & Systems, Inc.
Teradata is a trademark of NCR Corporation
UNIX is a trademark of the X/Open Company Limited
Visualizer is a trademark of International Business Machines Corporation
Visual Warehouse is a trademark of International Business Machines Corporation
Windows NT is a registered trademark of Microsoft Corporation

SECTION 1

INTRODUCING THE DATA WAREHOUSE

*According to a study by the META Group,
over 90% of its 2,000 Fortune 500
customers are considering adding data warehouse technology to their operations.*

Will your technology enable you to compete?

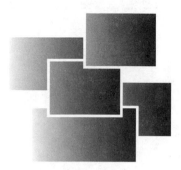

Chapter 1

REALITY AND THE VISION: EXECUTIVE OVERVIEW

Historically, businesses have weighted and valued information in proportion to the information's value in completing a transaction. Today, companies able to effectively organize and analyze the enormous amounts of data available can understand, interpret, and act on market dynamics—tremendously increasing their competitive advantage. The critical component of any corporation's strategy to analyze and organize this data is the *data warehouse*.

In this chapter, we first identify what a data warehouse is and the role it will play in your organization. We then discuss how to obtain a return on your

Because a data warehouse crosses many lines of business and political footholds within an organization, it is critical for an executive sponsor (from outside the information technology area) to champion the data warehouse throughout its implementation.

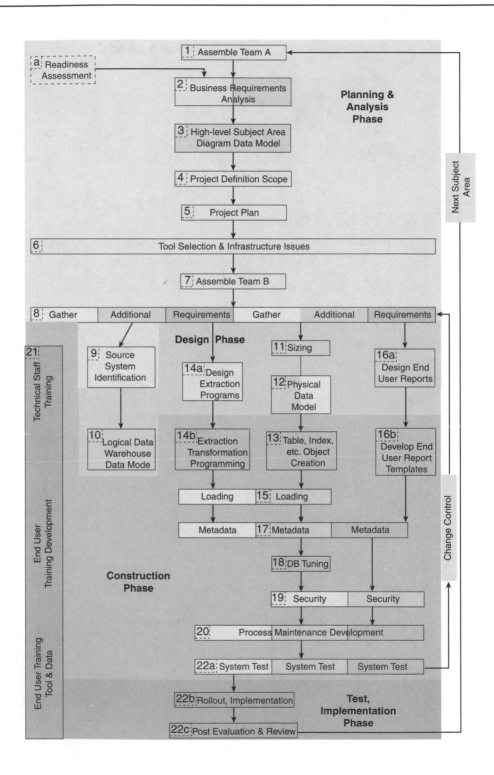

data warehouse investment, how to integrate and leverage the Internet, and what steps your data warehouse team will take to build the data warehouse. We also include factors critical to the success of the warehouse that will enable you to service your existing customers better and find new customers more easily.

The strength of the data warehouse is its organization and delivery of data in support of management's decision-making process. The data warehouse is the physical implementation of a relational or multidimensional decision support model which gives your enterprise the information it needs to make strategic decisions. A data warehouse supports business analyses and decision-making by integrating data from multiple, incompatible systems into a consolidated database. This transformation of data into meaningful information allows employees to perform more substantive, accurate, and consistent analyses.

Understanding and managing information is crucial for companies to make timely decisions and respond to changing business conditions. Because data processing applications proliferate across a variety of operating systems, the task of locating and integrating data for decision support is complicated. And, as employees throughout the enterprise are empowered with decision-making authority, more and more people need access to the information necessary for making business decisions. As a result of this paradigm shift, many organizations are building data warehouses to manage and use information efficiently and competitively.

Data warehousing equips users with more effective decision support tools by integrating enterprisewide corporate data into a single repository from which business end-users can run reports and perform ad hoc data analysis. Significant cost benefits, time savings, and productivity gains result from using a data warehouse for information processing. Data is easily accessed and analyzed without time-consuming manipulation and processing—freeing information technology staff and other resources. Decisions are made more quickly with confidence because the data is both timely and accurate. Information is consolidated into meaningful categories specified by users. Trends can be analyzed and predicted using historical data. And, the data warehouse ensures that everyone is using the same data at the same level of extraction, which eliminates conflicting analytical results and arguments over the source and quality of data. The data warehouse enables information processing to be done in a reliable, efficient manner.

Understanding the Role of the Data Warehouse

The first goal of a data warehouse is to enhance overall data availability. The second goal of the data warehouse is to enable a company to make strategic business decisions by enabling end-users to view information in a timely manner. And, the third goal of the data warehouse is to decrease information technology resources required to build and maintain reports.

Prior to my implementation of the data warehouse at CompuAdd, marketing and sales managers put in information requests to the information technology staff for reports and information. The staff would receive a request, size the effort, and report back as to the time required to construct the report. The report would then be constructed. Typically, marketing and sales staff received the information they needed two to three weeks *after* the fact. After implementing a data warehouse, sales teams and marketing staff (with training) used Cognos' sophisticated end-user ad hoc query and analysis tools to create custom reports within 15-30 minutes. The data warehouse was updated twice a day. The marketing and sales management now had current information when they needed the information, rather than receiving reports two to three weeks too late. What was critical to making this transformation in information delivery? We identified and acquired an easy-to-use end-user access tool, we defined 100% of the meta data and made it accessible, and we reproduced specific reports from the data warehouse (for example, market trends) daily. Meta data is the key to a successful warehouse. It provides the base for building, managing, and maintaining the data warehouse. See Section 2 for more information on meta data.

In the process of implementing a data warehouse, you'll inadvertently participate in your company's re-engineering processes by highlighting poor-quality data. Fortunately (or unfortunately for some), the data warehouse only transfers data; it doesn't change, modify, or improve the data. The only way to fix bad data is for both data entry personnel and management to modify the data at the source system. Be aware that your data warehouse team will probably go ahead and publish incomplete data. Pressure within the organization to modify the data will result when people recognize the implications of bad data and the value of good information.

> The ultimate goal of data warehousing is the creation of a single, logical view of an enterprise's data (typically residing in disparate physical databases), accessible by developers and business users alike.

The re-engineering of information systems attempts to deal with a production environment built an application at a time, in response to the business requirements of the moment, and maintained with application-specific fixes. One of the first tasks in building a data warehouse (as well as in process re-engineering) is to create data and process models representing the business' perspective of information and information processing. The data models are then used to reshape the production environment. Because of the chasm between the vision and reality, applying the data and process models to the production environment is a far cry from creating the data and process models in the first place. Using the data warehouse as the first step in re-engineering simplifies and streamlines the production environment (the volume of historical data is reduced by moving it to the data warehouse).

Extract from...
"Purina Mills Warehouses A Legacy Of Success"
Harding, Elizabeth. Software Magazine, n12, v15, Nov, 1995 p39(5)
Purina Mills' data warehouse implementation illustrates both the risks and the benefits the technology can bring to a company. Purina Mills sees the data warehouse as its first step in a migration to client/server computing and one that will let the company make the move in its own time. The company's decision was also influenced by its need to make data from a number of legacy systems available to more users. The new data warehouse had accessibility problems at first, because while more employees had access to it, few knew how to take advantage of it. Managers did not want their employees spending time learning programs, so in-house programs had to be developed to create smart end-user applications...
Growth and change, driven by business decisions, left the company with a lot of legacy software systems. As a result, Purina Mills' information systems staff has had to deal with a variety of business applications, many of which were written in-house over a 25-year period. The firm is a traditional MVS/CICS/Cobol mainframe site. Though they are evolving toward a client/server architecture, officials acknowledge that the effort is a long-term proposition since key applications can't be implemented overnight. Problems associated with replacing legacy systems require a long-term capital commitment, expensive training, recruitment programs and time. More than three years ago, when Purina Mills determined that its legacy general ledger system could no longer supply the business with all the required reporting and analysis options, the company began its search for a solution. The firm developed a financial reporting application based on data warehousing technology supplied by SAS Institute Inc., Cary, N.C.
While still running on the mainframe, Purina Mills' old general ledger system now has a prolonged lease on life. Data is now stored in SAS files on a UNIX-based IBM RS/6000 with a 12GB hard disk and 512MB of memory. Purina Mills put AIX on a Token-Ring network running TCP/IP with an X Windows interface. Users run OS/2 on the client and AIX on the server.

Excerpt from Purina Mills (continued)
Now, Purina Mills users can access the warehouse for ad hoc queries. The IS staff acknowledges that the idea of using a data warehouse for ad hoc queries is not new, but note that the costs of using a non-host platform are substantially lower than traditional mainframe means. The Purina Mills data warehouse has become a company-wide resource containing information from the corporate general ledger, sales and marketing, budget and billing applications. Extending the data warehouse beyond the UNIX platform with an EIS/DSS system gave users the ability to build their own mini data warehouse. This allowed them to extract data from the warehouse on one platform and download it for analysis/reporting. Instead of monthly paper reports which, in the past, trailed the close of a month by 10 to 15 days, the staff now get specific, important reports on a daily basis.

Determining Your Return on Investment (ROI)

With the addition of a data warehouse, you will immediately improve the productivity of your information technology staff. Since data warehousing automates information reporting processes and reduces programming, information technology professionals can focus on more pressing business issues (for example, IBM's Global Service organization can focus on migrating 200,000 Office Vision mail users to Lotus Notes). Also, your end-users can now run their own data marts, further reducing the information technology staff's workload.

Data warehousing enables non-technical users to link to current, usable information. This improves productivity and timeliness by putting the end-user in charge of the information. By taking advantage of this timely, accurate data and simpler end-user tools, decision-makers can discover new ways to increase revenue, reduce costs, attract new customers, and keep current customers more satisfied. Via information processing, your company will:

- Equip managers and business analysts with on-demand connectivity to the data warehouse
- Provide end-users with consistent data
- Enable data to be viewed in any possible combination or combinations, by every possible measure and/or dimension

What about the cost justification? To complete a typical ROI analysis requires that the benefits of a data warehouse be known prior to it being built.

Justification of dollars spent on data warehousing technologies is not so easy, because you can't make a simple cost-saving calculation. The specific benefits of the data warehouse are not known at the time of construction because the end-user cannot totally identify the possibilities and potentials until the first subject area is built. Companies garner their ROI from the data warehouse when the end-user accesses the data warehouse, learns what data is available, and starts to unlock the potential of the data warehouse. As with most development investment, data warehouse costs can be recurring or initial. Initial costs include hardware, software, and consulting services; recurring costs include licensing, maintenance, and resources. (Note that initial costs apply to each subject area iteration.) Because a data warehouse is built one subject area at a time, high initial expenditures are followed by successively lower expenditures as the design of the warehouse settles. Companies can control the data warehouse budget by building the warehouse incrementally and by encouraging end-users to use the data warehouse at the highest level of summarization.

You will undoubtedly face obstacles in populating your data warehouse. Typically, operational data is designed for applications that handle one record at a time. This format doesn't support quick queries. Empowered end-users frequently querying data in a high-volume, real-time OLTP (online transaction processing) environment will negatively impact your hardware and network performance. And, the very acts of querying and analyzing data will produce additional data that will need to be saved (resulting in the data warehouse needing its own DBMS (database management system) storage and hardware environment). Also, end-users can now create subsets, combinations, or aggregations of operational data; and historical data can now be accessed (which may also be grouped into subsets, aggregated, or combined in new ways), which will require additional storage.

The administrative and production sides of business have been well served by OLTP for the past 30 years. Today's technology, however, is focused on delivering tools to sales, marketing, and distribution teams desperate for a competitive advantage. Thirty years ago, production line efficiency was the key to business success; now, sales and marketing flexibility and responsiveness are critical to cultivating customers. When combined with a worldwide communications infrastructure, organizations that have harnessed the power of information will have a massive competitive advantage over their rivals.

Leveraging the Internet

By providing easy access to data, the Internet brings the same benefit to the data warehouse that it does to other business applications. The value of a data warehouse is maximized when the right data is in the hands of those who need it, regardless of when and where they need it. Today's client/server architecture spreads information across countless servers, leaving information technology groups struggling with giving end-users (particularly remote users) access to the right information. And, no matter how user-friendly the end-user access tool, users need training on how to use client applications.

The Web removes these issues by enabling easier access to data. More Web servers were sold for intranets in 1996 than were sold for external Internet use. Corporations discovered that the Web provides an efficient mechanism to realize the benefits of client/server architectures. Many of the same applications will work over the Internet, removing the complexity previously associated with supporting remote access. Finally, the client application is the same Web browser that is used for every other Web application, meaning that millions of people already know how to use it. Vendors are quickly providing new Web development tools that allow Web browsers to access data warehouses, including Arbor Software's Essbase Web Gateway, MicroStrategy's DSSWeb, and Information Advantage's WebOLAP.

Extract from... "Show Data Warehouse Benefits To End Users"
Braly, Damon. Health Management Technology, n11, v16, Oct, 1995 p22(3).
Disparate data sources prompted a warehouse solution for Tufts. Other signs indicating a need for a data warehouse included a reporting backlog, system functionality being limited by technology and the collection of data from multiple, disparate information sources. Tufts' information needs require the collection of data from disparate systems that are populated by the various health programs within Tufts Associated Health Plans. The health care system is the third largest Massachusetts-based managed-care company. The initial deployment of the data warehouse served as a model for other departments. Future users from other departments saw first hand how using the data warehouse in a live setting increased access to information.
Upon full system roll out, the benefits became even more pronounced. "We looked at the work request queue before and after installation to measure the efficacy of the effort," Shoup says. Almost a 50 percent reduction in report processing time was achieved. User buy in and use of the system surpassed expectations. The data warehouse brings Tufts into the information age, says Patricia Donovan, Tufts manager of PC and decision support. Data-hungry users make 20 times as many queries with the data warehouse in place. Users ordered 1,200 reports a year before the data warehouse. Now, users run 2,000 reports themselves each month. "With the old system, you had to fill out a work order and it often took 90 days to get the report," Donovan says. "Now if you ask a question, you can get an immediate response."

Building the Data Warehouse

> The data warehouse is a collection of integrated, subject-oriented databases designed to support the DSS (decision support system) function, where each unit of data is relevant to some moment in time.[a]

a. Inmon, W.H., *Building a Data Warehouse*, QED Technical Publishing Group, 1992.

The true value of this book is the methodology we present to design and deploy a data warehouse (see Figure 1-1). This methodology follows the typical system development life cycle (SDLC) design identified by the planning and analysis, design, construction, and testing and implementation phases. Because designing a data warehouse is an incremental process, the methodology reflects the incremental *subject area* construction. We've color-coded the methodology to enable quick identification of each technical team member's responsibility. In the chapters that follow, we focus on the specifics of each phase of the data warehouse deployment and include deliverables applicable to each step of the process.

We've highlighted what occurs in each step of the methodology below, identifying key players, requirements, and deliverables. You will find thorough discussions of each step in the chapters that follow.

The first phase, the Planning & Analysis Phase, encompasses the initial steps in building the data warehouse, including:

☐ **(1) Assemble Team A:** The project manager has the responsibility of assembling the initial team (including the data modeler, business analysts, and key business end-users) to determine business requirements and create the project definition and scope. This initial team will be responsible for completing the first five steps in this methodology, as well as identifying the subject area for the pilot data warehouse (discussed in Chapter 3).

☐ **(2) Determine Initial Business Requirements**: Start the project by gathering high-level data warehouse requirements and determining expectations with your power users, casual users, and end-users (discussed in Chapter 3).

☐ **(3) Build the High-level Subject Area Diagram:** Build a data model that represents a corporation's high level subject areas (or entities). This data model generally shows the subject areas and their relationships to each other, as well as definitions for each entity. One of these subject areas is generally chosen for your pilot (discussed in Chapter 5).

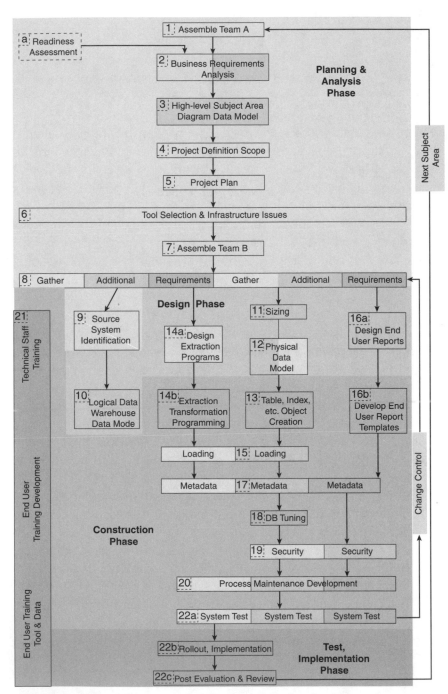

Figure 1-1 Methodology for designing, building, and deploying the data warehouse.

> Data naturally congregates around major categories relevant to the business. These categories are called subject areas, or high-level entities.

❑ **(4) Define the Project and Scope:** The project definition and scope function as the data warehouse business plan, identifying the project description, objectives, critical success factors, assumptions, and issues. Most importantly, the project definition and scope document sets expectations up front. The scope document will initially identify the pilot deployment (discussed in Chapter 3).

❑ **(5) Construct the Project Plan:** The project plan details the design and construction of the data warehouse. The plan consists of tasks for building the data warehouse, the time frame for each activity, deliverables, milestones, assigned resources, and costs (discussed in Chapter 3).

❑ **(6) Choose the Tools and Infrastructure:** Due to the complexity of the data warehouse infrastructure, we examine vendors and products in Chapter 4, evaluating, among other attributes, ease of use, performance, and vendor stability (discussed in Chapter 4).

❑ **(7) Assemble Team B:** After completing steps one through six, the rest of the team should be assembled to complete the remaining tasks in parallel (discussed in Chapter 3).

❑ **(8) Gather Additional Requirements:** This step differs from the initial requirements gathering because it is subject area-specific. For example, you would ask your sales organization: Where is information stored? Which is the system of record? What information do you want via the reports? What are your power user, casual user, and end-user expectations? Do you want daily transaction reports or weekly transaction reports? (discussed in Chapter 3.)

❑ **(8b) Determine End-User Report Requirements:** The data warehouse provides a source of reliable, accessible, well-defined and well-documented data. Provide tools to end-users that enable them to realize the value of the data (discussed in Chapter 9).

❑ **(9) Identify the Source System:** After the data model is built, identify and define the system of record (discussed in Chapter 5).

❑ **(10) Create the Logical Data Model:** After composing your high-level subject area diagram, create a logical data model, reflecting the attributes and entities for a selected data warehouse area. The logical data model captures all pertinent information about the selected entity (for example, a customer, an order, or an invoice). However, don't worry at this point about whether you're using a computerized, manual, or mechanical process for your data warehouse implementation. Use this step to gather information only (discussed in Chapter 5).

> The data warehouse is a data-driven development process. This approach centers around identifying a corporation's common enterprise data through a technique called data modeling. Typical data models begin with the high-level subject area diagram, followed by the mid-level data model (referred to as a DIS, or data item set), and the logical and physical data models. A data model is a system used to represent the relationships between data, sometimes referred to as an entity relationship diagram (ERD).

☐ **(11) Size the Data Warehouse:** Capacity planning in the data warehouse centers around disk storage and processing resources—the more data there is, the more processing power required. Disk storage capacity is a function of the level of detail stored, the length of time the data is kept, and the number of occurrences of data to be stored. Processor capacity is a function of the batch processing update window and concurrent ad hoc user's workload (discussed in Chapter 6).

☐ **(12) Build the Physical Data Model:** The DBA implements the physical data model, converting the logical data model into a physical model by removing operational-only data; adding time stamps, indexes, and referential integrity constraints; merging tables; and adding levels of summarization, aggregation, or derivations of data. Performance issues and end-user requirements will be inputs to this process (discussed in Chapter 6).

☐ **(13) Build the Database Management System (DBMS):** It's time to build the database and tables to house the data (discussed in Chapter 6).

☐ **(14a,b) Extract, Transform, and Scrub:** This is the process of mapping all data elements from the source systems to the data warehouse tables, typically requiring the transformation and merging of data from the source system (the OLTP) to the data warehouse (discussed in Chapter 7).

❐ **(15) Load the Data:** Load the data—which really means create, load, and optimize the DBMS, as well as schedule the processes for extracting, loading, scrubbing, and transferring the data to the data warehouse host, and then building summarization tables for performance (discussed in Chapter 6).

❐ **(16a,b) Develop End-user Tool Report Templates:** Ensure that the end-user queries, reporting, graphing, ad hoc requests, and analysis requirements are met via an off-the-shelf package or an in-house developed application (discussed in Chapter 9).

❐ **(17) Create the Repository for and Document the DBMS Meta Data:** Meta data catalogues the information stored in the data warehouse and the transformation performed on the data when it was transferred from the legacy systems (or OLTP systems) (discussed in Chapter 8).

❐ **(18) Tune the Database:** Tune the data loaded into the data warehouse for optimum performance of both batch loading and end-user access. Choose tools that identify problems and troublesome thresholds and apply corrective action (discussed in Chapter 6).

❐ **(19) Secure the Data:** The data warehouse is built for data access and is considered a failure if it cannot accommodate easy and unconstrained access. However, data security in the data warehouse requires that data access be limited and controlled (discussed in Chapter 6).

❐ **(20) Document Operation Processes and Procedures** (Discussed in Chapter 10).

❐ **(21) Train:** Train the end users to efficiently use the data access tool and educate them as to the implications of the data (discussed in Chapter 10).

❐ **(22a,b,c) Test, Rollout, and Follow Up**: Create a test plan, then implement, modify, and rollout to business analyst end-users. Next, conduct a post-project evaluation to determine where improvements could be made for the next data warehouse project. Also, review possible next projects to determine the best fit with the existing data (discussed in Chapter 10).

Critical Success Factors

It's simple (in theory) to make your data warehouse a success. If you keep the following rules in mind, you just might avoid the majority of the land mines:

• Recruit a sponsor for the data warehouse implementation to be the central coordinator and promoter. The sponsor's primary task is to champion the data warehouse concept inside your company.

- Develop a prototype rapidly. Success or failure of a data warehouse project is determined by how quickly users see the concrete value for the company as a whole.
- Protect any investment by beginning with a step-by-step implementation of the data warehouse. You'll be able to identify costs and modify the design of the project without sacrificing any work completed in the interim.
- Clearly identify your project structure and scope and set end-user expectations up-front.
- Create *flexible* requirements, including: cross-platform capability—new software, new hardware, and other operating systems must all be capable of being implemented inside the existing data warehouse solution; guaranteeing consolidated data material as the basis of all reports and analyses; and state-of-the-art tools like OLAP and neural networks, which facilitate creative reporting.
- Critically evaluate every piece of hardware and software and every tool to ensure that your ROI is guaranteed. You will be inundated with vendors and their products. Don't be fooled by lengthy presentations or dazzling technologies. Mandatory tools include: automated tools to capture design; an easy-to-use end-user access tool; a data extraction/transformation tool; a parallel, scalable RDBMS; and, scalable hardware.
- *And, along the way...* Address data integrity issues. Hire personnel who understand relational technology. Create a data model incorporating relational technology. Talk to your end-users—find out what it is they want out of the data warehouse and let them test potential systems. Once you have your prototype up and running, show the users. Measure work requests and response time before and after installation of the data warehouse.

We also recommend that you consult with independent industry experts. Visit their Web sites first and determine if they have the expertise your data warehouse implementation will require. For example, Prism, at http://www. prismsolutions.com, interactively permits visitors to register for seminars, ask questions, and participate in data warehousing chat forums. Visitors to the Prism home page can easily navigate their way through a variety of topics for information about data warehousing and Prism solutions. Select "Value of a Data Warehouse" to find out what a data warehouse is and how it enables better information management, analysis, and decision-making. Observations on the business benefits of data warehousing by industry analysts from the Aberdeen Group, Gartner Group, IDC, and META Group are included. There are also examples of customers' business applications in different vertical industries and their testimonials about the ROI provided by Prism products. Another link, "Products," provides an overview of Prism's entire product line, including: Prism Warehouse Manager, which automates the extraction, integration, and mapping of legacy and operational data to a data warehouse; Prism Directory Manager, which integrates business and technical meta data into an information directory for the warehouse; the Inmon Generic Data Models, which provide templates for data warehouse design; and, Prism's extensive consulting services.

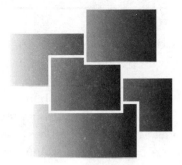

Chapter 2

DATA WAREHOUSING 101

Get ready—we're about to inundate you with the concepts, framework, and components you'll need to build your warehouse. Consider this your crash course in data warehousing…

Decision support is key for companies wanting to turn their organizational data into an informational asset. Why? Decision support provides the base for powerful, analytical and decision-making techniques. Decision support in the data warehousing environment (using data mining and multidimensional data analysis, coupled with parallel processing) can enhance the speed and accuracy at which decisions are made. Your data warehouse strategy must provide an end-to-end solution, consisting of access to many database sources and robust middleware tools, including meta data and decision support tools that offer scalable functionality to a broad set of users.

In this chapter, we'll define the data warehouse, then compare and contrast online analytical processing (OLAP) with online transaction processing (OLTP) applications. We'll focus on data storage and data warehouse architecture. A more detailed look will be taken at the data warehouse infrastructure, including parallel hardware, data extraction, transformation, and scrubbing, data storage, meta data, data access, and data delivery. We'll then identify the components of the data model and the role the pilot project plays in the data warehouse implementation.

What is a Data Warehouse?

We'll start with a nod to Bill Inmon (frequently referred to as the father of data warehousing)—according to Bill Inmon, a data warehouse is subject-oriented, integrated, nonvolatile, and time-variant[1]. What does this mean?

❐ Subject-oriented
   Within any business, data naturally congregates around categories or subject areas. Data warehouses are built around these broad, non-overlapping subjects rather than around a business process, system, or function. For example, subject areas are Customer, Order, Product, and Vendor, while business processes are Customer Billing, Order Entry, and Accounts Payable.
❐ Integrated
   Data is integrated by datawide consistencies in the measurement of variables, naming conventions, and physical data definitions—for example, there is only one definition, one identifier, and one characteristic attribute.

Figure 2–1 illustrates how an individual's checking account, savings account, and investment account information can be integrated and transformed into one view.

---

1. Inmon, W.H., Imhoff, C., and Battas, G., *Building the Operational Data Store*, John Wiley and Sons, New York, 1996.

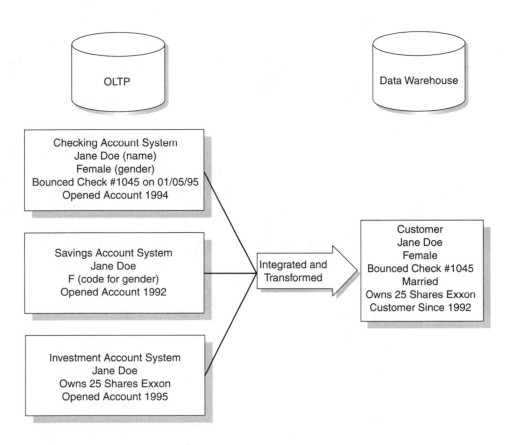

Figure 2–1 Data integration.

□ Time-variant
   Historical and accurate at some point in time, data in a data warehouse is a
   "snapshot" of an organization's information. Data warehouse data is
   extracted from operational systems that enable it to be archived. This archival and subsequent historical value gives data warehouses an element of
   time as part of their structure.

□ Nonvolatile
   Since the data in the data warehouse is a snapshot of a corporation's data at
   a specific point in time, the data shouldn't be changed, modified, or
   updated. The data is stored for its value at that point in a corporation's history. What if the data isn't correct? Then the data in the operational system
   was not correct—correct the data in the operational application and take a
   new snapshot of the data warehouse.

OLAP versus OLTP Applications

Information retrieval applications are typically characterized as either operational (OLTP) or decision support (OLAP). The OLTP environment was created to support a high volume of rapid transactions—the day-to-day business of your company. The OLAP environment, on the other hand, was designed to provide information used for analyzing a problem or situation. OLAP is primarily done by comparing or analyzing patterns and trends. Unlike operational software, which is designed for automating day-to-day operations like capturing, validating, and storing large numbers of individual transactions, decision support systems help managers make better decisions by analyzing summarized snapshots of corporate performance. Traditional operational systems are very good at putting data into databases quickly, accurately, and efficiently, but are not very good at delivering meaningful analyses in return. Characteristics of each environment are highlighted in Table 2–1.

Table 2–1 OLTP vs. OLAP

System Characteristics	OLTP	OLAP
User interaction required?	Transactions only	Throughout the entire database
How much data is affected?	Individual records	Groups of information
What is my response time?	Seconds	Seconds to minutes
What is the machine utilization?	Consistent	Dynamic
How is the data characterized?	Detailed data	Summary data
How do I access the data?	In a predefined way	Any way you want
What are the overall system priorities?	Optimized for performance and availability	Optimized for flexible end-user interaction
The database is configured for...	Transaction updates	Queries
The database is optimized for...	Bulk transactions	Analysis
How much maintenance does the data require?	Updated frequently	Minimal updates

OLAP enables users to view and analyze data across multiple dimensions. Decision-makers can ask questions that are business-oriented, involving trends, comparisons, and consolidations that span several business facts/dimensions over a given period of time. Typical OLAP operations include *rollup* (increasing the level of detail), and *drill-down* (decreasing the level of detail), along one or more dimension hierarchies, *slice-and-dice* (selection and projection), and *pivot* (reorienting the multidimensional view of data).[2]

Multidimensional OLAP database access tools organize data by classifying it in business terms. This is the most natural way to view an organization as a whole, because it is based on the business structure, not computer constructs. For example, sales may be classified by product sold, the customer who bought it, when the sale occurred, the location, the value, and the volume. This naturally fits into a multidimensional structure with products, customers, time, geography, and measures as dimensions. Facts begin to provide meaning to decision-makers when they are surrounded by these business dimensions; for example, decision-makers can ask, "Compared to the previous year, how have the last 12 months of increased advertising expenditures impacted my product's sales in New York compared to San Francisco?" Figure 2–2 illustrates the many dimensions accessible via this structure.

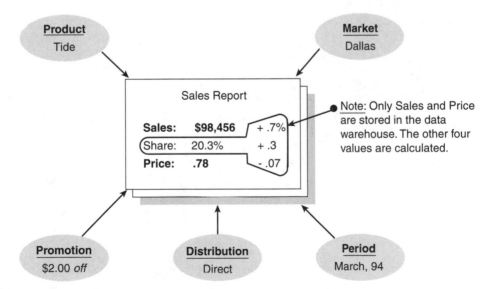

Figure 2–2 Multidimensional sales report.

2. Chaudhuri, S., Dayal, U., "An Overview of Data Warehouse and OLAP Technology," *SIGMOD*, Vol. 26, No. 1, March 1997, pp. 65-74.

Table 2–2 below illustrates the business logic layer included with OLAP that SQL query tools are less efficient at obtaining.

Table 2–2 Advantages of Using Business Logic

OLAP Business Logic	Example
Ratios	Brand to category index
Comparisons	Volume % change vs. year ago
Rankings	Top ten by market
Consolidations	Price, share, weighted average
Cross-dimensional calculations	Shared by customer groupings across dimensions over time

One issue with OLAP has been its complete lack of standards. There are no standards for: defining calculations, creating structures, reporting, and benchmarking. If you like a vendor's multidimensional database, you must also buy its report writer, end-user access tool, and/or data access tools. However, the OLAP Council,[3] established in January 1995, plans to provide:

- Education on OLAP technology for business
- Standard definitions and terms
- Interoperability standards and technologies

Multidimensional Data Storage

There are two ways of storing multidimensional data. The multidimensional database (MDD) uses proprietary cubes for storing data (also referred to as multidimensional online analytical processing, or MOLAP), as illustrated in Figure 2–3.

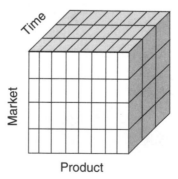

Figure 2–3 Multidimensional database (MDD).

3. http://www.olapcouncil.org

The other method of storing multidimensional data utilizes a standard relational database management system (RDBMS), where the data is stored using a star schema. In the star schema, the database consists of a single fact table and a single table for each dimension (see Figure 2–4).

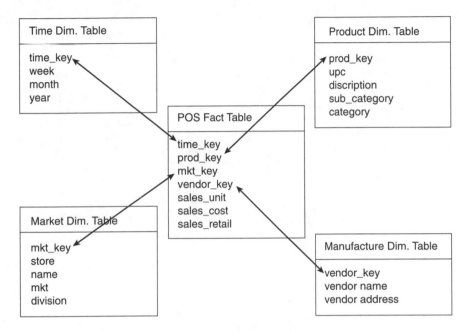

Figure 2–4 Star schema.

Data Warehouse Architecture

Typically, an OLAP system utilizes a data warehouse design or architecture. In this context the *data warehouse* has been linked to Excel spreadsheets, to multi-dimensional databases, and to terabyte detailed-data data mining using genetic algorithms—and these are all valid data warehouses, as illustrated by the layers of the data warehouse architecture shown in Figure 2–5.

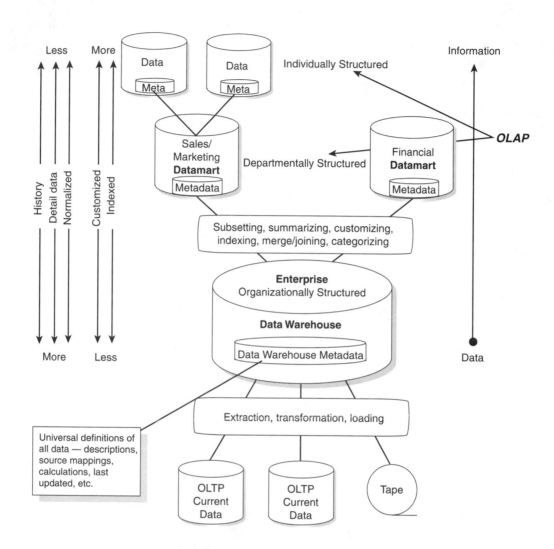

Figure 2–5 OLAP in the data warehouse architecture.

OLTP, or **legacy system data,** is detailed and up-to-date—*for example,* order entry and banking transactions. Consistency and recoverability of the database is critical, and maximizing transaction throughput is the critical performance metric.

Extracting and transforming data from the source system to the enterprise involves the integration of sources illustrated in the above diagram, transformation of codes, conflicting data types, and adding the element of time.

Enterprise, organizationally-structured, atomic data is granular data that reflects a time variant and is integrated, subject-oriented data (this is usually where *data mining* activities take place—see Chapter 9). Organizationally-structured enterprise data must take into consideration the need for control and the integrity of the data being integrated and transformed from the various production sources. Any performance requirements on this atomic level of data must be directed towards the population of the data warehouse from production sources. The end-user interface to the organizationally structured data is much cruder, and the activities in this environment are to select and gather data. Analysts usually use complex procedural tools for statistical analysis and data mining.

Departmentally-structured data, the *data mart,* is data summarized by department (for example, accounting, marketing, and manufacturing) from the atomic, detailed level. It is often characterized by a star schema for multidimensional OLAP analysis. The multidimensional database (MDD) can often be used at this level if the size is under 50GB. Note that the MDD structure and associated analysis tools are often much easier and faster to implement and should be considered where *update* versus *read only* is desired (for example, for *What if?* scenarios in planning).

An alternative to the detailed, organizationally-structured enterprise data warehouse and the highly summarized, departmentally-structured data mart is the **data mart-only** architecture. Many companies are bypassing the organizationally-structured enterprise data warehouse and heading for the data mart. These companies either store the detail data in their fact tables in the star schema data mart design, or they summarize and load the data mart database from their legacy online transaction systems. (See Chapter 4 for more information on data marts.)

Basically, the data mart is a subset of a larger data warehouse. Departmental data marts are typically reconcilable since all share the same source data; however, the organizational detail enterprise data. Often the OLAP departmental data marts run on different hardware platforms optimized for them rather than the organizational data platform. This also distributes the work load, increasing performance. You also limit the scope of what you're trying to achieve with a data mart, making the solution simpler to understand and maintain. Finally, there is the autonomy issue. Data marts break up the data warehouse, allowing each group of users to manipulate the data separately.

Operational data warehouses (or operational data stores) move in the opposite direction. Rather than portioning off smaller pieces of the data warehouse, they combine the data warehouse with traditional OLTP operational systems. These systems allow users to analyze the data and then take real-time actions, all within the same system. For example, you can look at recent purchasing patterns and, based on that analysis, enter transactions to ship products to appropriate stores. Or, you might analyze stock price trends and then issue buy and sell orders within the same system. In addition, the resources expended on extracting data from the operational system can be reduced because the warehouse and operational system are no longer two separate systems.

Essentially, data marts further replicate data and decentralize access, and operational data warehouses further consolidate data and centralize access. Data marts will flourish because people like to have decentralized control over their own data. And, automatic tools are being developed that will help keep the information in data marts current and consistent with the data in the enterprise-level data warehouse. Remember, however, that sooner or later, the data in a data mart will be of interest to outside users--so consider corporate standards for hardware, software, networking, database management systems, and naming conventions.

The **individually structured database** is optional and is used to even further summarize or parcel data from the department data mart into data the individual performing the analysis is interested in. This data is usually stored on the analyst's PC and is considered temporary, ad hoc only storage.

Data Warehouse Infrastructure

Open architecture in decision support tools is critical. The warehouse must support every conceivable type of query and investigation that can be imagined if the decision support function is to perform effectively. Existing tools, such as spreadsheets and preferred query and reporting tools, should also be supported.

When creating the data warehouse infrastructure, the data warehouse architect will have to:

- Define the implementation requirements and technical infrastructure for a client server architecture
- Understand how to gather and store meta data
- Choose the correct hardware and software
- Choose an appropriate network configuration
- Develop an application methodology and applications appropriate for the data warehouse
- Understand critical success factors for migrating to a data warehouse environment
- Provide ongoing support for the data warehouse

To accomplish these objectives, the data warehouse architect must possess the following skills:

- Education in DSSs
- Data transformation tool training
- Operating system expertise
- Database expertise
- Expertise in data warehouse database design
- Data access tool training
- Meta data navigation training

Building the data warehouse infrastructure requires time. New hardware and software often needs to be purchased and installed; data transformation tools must be reviewed and chosen; and networks, gateways, and communications must be set up. Note that the infrastructure should be chosen and in the process of being installed before data warehouse development begins. Infrastructure costs typically fit into the overall data warehouse project as illustrated in Figure 2–6.

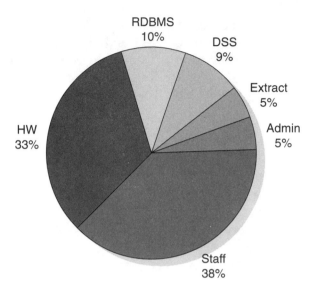

Figure 2–6 Data warehouse cost breakdown.

Parallel Hardware

Parallel hardware architecture enables system expansion by allowing incremental processor upgrades without the need for complete system upgrades. Parallel hardware allows complex queries to be run against vast quantities of historical data, providing organizations with topical trends and patterns not previously achievable within a reasonable time frame. Parallel hardware enables performance-critical data processing applications to quickly respond in a volatile market. However, parallel technology is exploited only if the software and complementary hardware support is in place.

Architectures for parallel processing can exploit the use of multiple processors, large amounts of memory, and multiple disk storage units. The most common architectures are shared-nothing, shared-disks, and shared-memory.

❑ Shared-nothing: Referred to as loosely coupled or massively parallel processing (MPP); uses multiple processors, each with its own memory and disk storage units

❑ Shared-disks: Uses multiple processors, each with its own memory, but shares disk storage units

❑ Shared-memory: Referred to as tightly coupled or symmetric multiprocessors (SMP); uses multiple processors that have common memory and share disk storage units

With shared-nothing, each individual processor has its own private memory and access to its own disks. The processors communicate via message passing. IBM's RS/6000 SP is an example of hardware with this architecture; DB2 Parallel Edition also takes advantage of this architecture. Oracle, Sybase, and Informix produce parallel versions of their databases as well.

MPP platforms enable platforms to scale from only a few processors to hundreds, if not thousands, of processors, allowing incremental growth that can be combined with the gradual growth of the data warehouse.

When considering your architecture, remember *data access middleware.* Middleware (which provides gateway or copy management functionality) enables connectivity to heterogeneous servers and networks during data warehouse population and connects end-users to the warehouse in a transparent and easily managed way. For example, IBM's Data Propagator enables copy management or data extraction, data transformation, replication, and propagation. IBM's Datajoiner works as a gateway, accessing DB2, as well as other databases (other products, including Cross Access, are DBMS-independent middleware applications, enabling access to different vendors' RDBMSs).[4]

Data Extraction, Transformation, and Scrubbing

Data acquisition includes *extracting* data from operational systems, scrubbing the data (restructuring records, translating field values to a common data dictionary, and checking data integrity and consistency), *transformating* the data (adding time fields, summarizing data, and deriving new fields), *and loading* the "clean" data into the warehouse database, as well as updating the warehouse's indexes.

Data Storage

Data storage represents the database and accompanying structures which are used in the analytical process. Relational and multidimensional databases are primarily used in architectures today, and while there is a fair amount of debate in the industry as to which provides the best results, relational databases offer more flexibility, smaller overall size, and easier access to atomic data for drill-down operations. As a result, database vendors are adding multidimensional functions to relational products.

---

4. For a thorough discussion of middleware in the data warehouse environment, see "Middleware: Gluing the Warehouse Together," by Susan Gausden and Terry Mason, pp. 252–273, in *Data Warehouse: Practical Advice from the Experts*, editors Joyce Bischoff and Ted Alexander, Prentice Hall, 1997.

Meta Data

Meta data reflects the data warehouse inventory; and, the meta data repository houses the meta data characteristics. The meta data repository gives users and technicians information about the data, such as: Where did the data come from? What rules were used in creating the data? and, What do the data elements mean? Many systems separate the business or end-user directory (such as IBM's DataGuide) from the development directory (such as IBM's Visual Warehouse), so that technical information about the data, which would be of limited use to an end-user, and could arguably make the end-user's task more difficult, is kept in a separate directory from that which is required by the user to understand the data from a business perspective.

Data Access

The tools presented to the end-user are the ones which will ultimately drive their perception of the utility of the system. Access can be categorized as: standard query, data interpretation, mutidimensional analysis, and/or data mining. *Standard query* tools allow users to develop a hypothesis and create questions (queries) to test the validity of the hypothesis. This is sometimes called a *verification-driven* approach. *Data interpretation* tools support advanced analysis of data, for example, business statistics and optimization (linear programming). *Multidimensional analysis* tools facilitate flexible investigation of the data along various dimensions, applying operations such as time series analyses, and enabling interactive *drill-down* capabilities. *Data mining* tools use a discovery-driven approach to detect trends, patterns, and correlations hidden in the data.

Data Delivery

Data delivery is how the data is presented to the end-user, including both the conduit by which it reaches the end-user and the mechanisms for visualizing the data. Geographic dispersion, security, and data volumes dictate the use of local area networks, the Internet, and/or wide area networks (public and private). Query complexity and output volume dictate the rendering of the data. Options range from simple tables (such as spreadsheets), to simple two-dimensional graphics (such as bar graphs and pie charts), to very sophisticated visualization technologies which utilize three-dimensional landscapes to portray the results.

Understanding the Data Model

Data warehouse teams are usually under quite a bit of pressure to get the warehouse up and running. One of the first steps you'll probably want to skip is building a data model. Don't even think about it! The biggest issue associated with the construction of a data warehouse is understanding the data. Creating a data model is the best way to understand the data.

> A data model represents the definition, characterization, and relationships of data in a given environment. It serves as a blueprint for building a solid data warehouse foundation.

The data model ensures:

- Completeness of scope (think of it as your blueprint, guiding development over the long haul)
- Interlocking parts (the data model keeps track of the intertwining parts found in large, complex data warehouses)
- A solid foundation for future additions
- Identification of redundant data

The four levels of data models to develop when building a data warehouse include (illustrated in Figure 2–7)[5]:

1. High-level/Subject Area Logical Model—A data model of the information used in an organization from an end-user's perspective, without regard to its functional or physical aspects.

2. Mid-level Logical Model—Contains the structure of the information, including details about what will be connected to what and how.

3. Data Warehouse/Dimensional Model—A data model configured to reflect the usage of data for decision support analysis.

4. Physical Data Model—The data definition language (DDL), which depicts the storage parameters, index clause, and referential integrity (primary key and foreign key relationships).

5. For additional information on data modeling, see Inmon, W.H., *Building a Data Warehouse*, QED Technical Publishing Group, 1992.

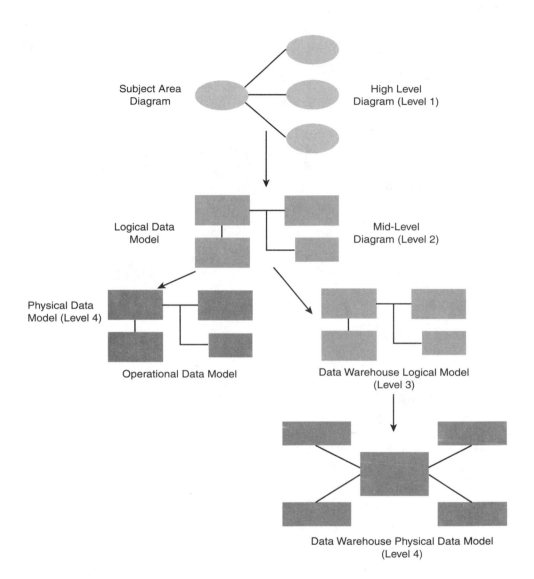

Figure 2–7 Relationship between the high-level, mid-level, data warehouse, and physical models.

Steps 1, 2, and 4 of the model architecture have historically been discussed in entity relationship diagram (ERD) modeling, as they related to transaction processing systems. Since data warehouses are developed with analytical processing in mind, we have added the concept of the data warehouse/dimensional model. This model represents the information along multidimensional lines.

The first step, the corporate high-level subject area data model, is the best place to start with the process of building a data warehouse. For the transformation from the corporate data model to the data warehouse data model to occur, the corporate data model must identify and structure:

- The major subjects of the enterprise
- The relationships between the subjects
- A high-level ERD

Data naturally congregates around major categories relevant to the business. These categories are called *subject areas,* or *high-level entities.* Within a subject area diagram, data is categorized into broad, fundamentally different, non-overlapping areas; the major relationships of data have been identified, and the commonality of data across the environment has been recognized. The benefits of the subject area diagram include:

- The ability to perceive the enterprise at the highest level of abstraction
- The ability to view the impact of future developments on the basic building blocks of the organization
- The ability to view these basic components of the enterprise independent of political or parochial perspectives

The high-level data model looks like Figure 2–8.

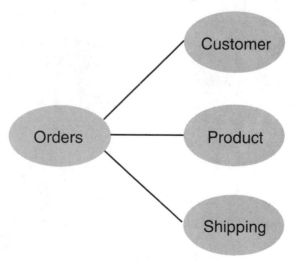

Figure 2–8 A simple high-level model.

There are many indirect relationships inferred from the high-level data model, but only the direct relationships are shown. The high-level data model does not contain any amount of detail because detail would only clutter it. The high-level data model can cover the entire enterprise (referred to as an enterprise data model), or it can have a restricted scope.

The mid-level data model contains the details, including the keys, attributes, subtypes, groupings, attributes, and connectors. For each high-level subject area identified, there is a single mid-level model. Do not try to put any thought into how the information will be retrieved or what it will be used for. All that will come later. At this time, simply focus on the structure of the information—the attributes and relations between them. The relationship between each subject area identified in the high-level model and the mid-level model is shown in Figure 2–9.

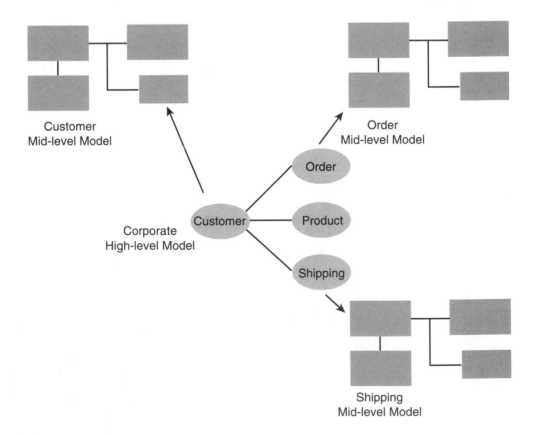

Figure 2–9 Each subject area has its own mid-level data model.

Traditional logical data modeling, such as the development of ERDs, is sometimes applied to data warehouse development projects. This typically occurs if your corporation requires the model to be in the corporate CASE tool before creating any physical tables in any database. Data warehouse projects can be successful with a complete and accurate physical star schema dimensional business model.

The Pilot Project

Fortunately, data warehouses are built incrementally. The first iteration can be done quickly and for a relatively small amount of money. Once the first subject area is built and populated, the analyst can start to explore the possibilities. As such, the OLAP development process is nearly the reverse of the traditional OLTP development process (see Figure 2–10).

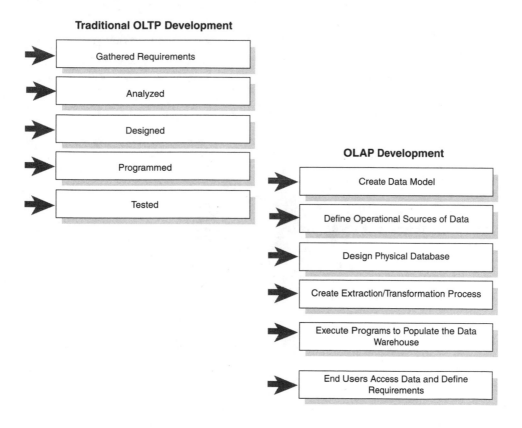

Figure 2–10 Development process comparison.

To ensure a successful pilot project, you need to both clarify the purpose of the project and treat the pilot as a development project (allocate the appropriate resources and a project manager). The pilot will help your team understand the complexities involved in developing a data warehouse, gain experience with new tools and technologies, get a sense of realistic timelines, and understand the learning curves for tasks and tools. Note that the pilot will be refined and enhanced when moving on to the next subject area.

Use the high-level subject area diagram to select the appropriate subject area for the pilot. The first iteration should contain data that is large enough to be meaningful, but small enough to be quickly populated into the data warehouse and analyzed. You can:

- Implement a single subject area (best option)
- Implement a subset of a subject area
- Implement a subset of several subject areas (most common)

You can also consider what drives the revenues for your company, such as sales, finance, or marketing, and then choose one of these areas for the pilot. The most common data warehouse applications are identified in Figure 2–11. If possible, work with a business area or department that is excited about the project and getting access to information.

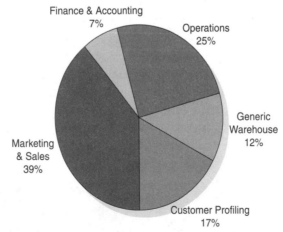

Source: Bruce Love, *Strategic Data Warehouse*, Journal of Data Warehousing, July 1996, p. 37.

Figure 2–11 Data warehouse applications (Gartner Group, Percy/Strange).

SECTION 2

MANAGING THE DATA WAREHOUSE

According to the Gartner Group, "The heat is on. . . to get data warehouses up and running fast" [but] "The biggest benefit comes down the road, when you can support 20 different decision support applications with the same architecture."

Are we there yet?

39

Chapter 3

IT'S JUST BUSINESS: DATA WAREHOUSE PROJECT MANAGEMENT

Data warehouse projects frequently experience difficulty because the project manager and team members fail to perceive the size, scope, and complexity of building the data warehouse. Traditional informational technology skills, such as planning and design, and an up-front investment of time and effort, are critical for deploying large data warehouse projects.

When implemented efficiently and expertly—just follow the included directions—a data warehouse can offer tremendous benefits to your organization.

41

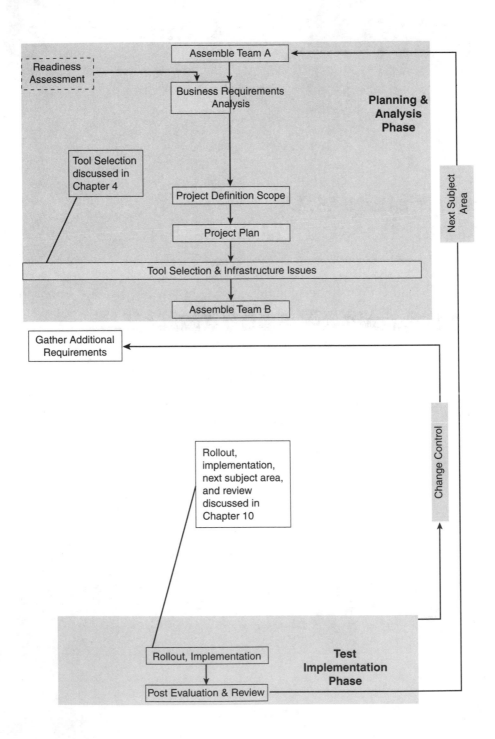

Delivering timely, accurate information to your organization requires:

- Accessing a variety of data sources for populating your data warehouse
- Transforming the data into information using tools for cleansing, summarizing, and aggregating source data before placing it in the data warehouse
- Distributing the information to the locations where it makes the most sense for satisfying users' needs and makes the best use of your processing and storage resources
- Storing your data, including multidimensional and multimedia objects, on industrial-strength database management systems
- Managing and automating data warehouse processes to maintain control and minimize operational resource requirements
- Finding and understanding the information in the data warehouse and understanding exactly what the warehouse information means in business terms
- Displaying, analyzing, and discovering the information and using it for business decision-making

This chapter focuses on the initial steps to be taken by the project manager to accomplish the above tasks, including assembling the initial team, conducting readiness assessment(s), determining the initial business requirements, organizing the project plan and scope, building the project plan, assembling the support team, and assembling additional business requirements. We'll first assemble the team and then move forward to understand and complete the subsequent tasks.

Assembling the Initial Team

The project team must be cross-functional, consisting of members with a diverse range of technical and business skills. Different team members will need to take a lead role at different times since each phase places different demands on the skills and expertise of the team members.

It is the project manager's responsibility to assemble an initial team to determine the business requirements and put together the project definition and scope. This initial team typically consists of the data modeler, business analyst, and key business end-users. This team will be responsible for completing the first five steps in this methodology, as well as identifying the subject area for the pilot data warehouse. Supporting the data warehousing staff with the right training, consulting help, motivation, and definition of roles and responsibilities helps ensure a smooth project rollout. The skills sets and job responsibilities necessary to maintain the warehouse are varied and complex. And, they are coupled with tools and methodologies that are sometimes experimental and often introduced to an uninitiated team. Supporting the warehouse also requires a fundamental change in mindset and values—moving from a mainframe-centric environment to the world of client/server, from controlled access to free-form access, from limited distribution to broad access, and from structured applications to ad hoc access in an unstructured environment.

To help foster this new mindset quickly, organizations should make a point to select the best and the brightest of the organization for the warehouse team. These individuals may come from different disciplines, such as business analysis, data modeling, data administration, applications development, end-user support, or the corporation's information technology group. Proper training, mentoring, planning, motivation, organization, and patience can help ensure that the data warehousing team is positioned to provide the highest level of support, thereby returning the highest return on investment to the organization. Avoid disaster by clearly identifying the critical roles, responsibilities, and organizational structure as illustrated in Figure 3–1.

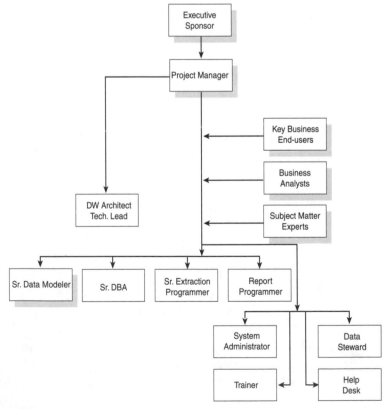

Figure 3–1 Team members critical to the data warehouse project (team members assembled initially are indicated via shadowing).

The organization and composition of the data warehouse team can be configured in numerous ways depending upon your organizational processes, management structure, and distribution of resources. We recommend organizing the following team initially to get the project rolling:

❏ **Executive/Corporate Sponsor**: Sponsorship at the executive level is necessary to make the warehouse a priority within the organization.

❏ **Project Manager**: Project management of the warehouse team is needed to ensure that the warehouse is aligned with the business needs and to develop project plans to support the warehouse as it matures. The project manager manages the overall project, performs project reviews, works to accomplish the project tasks identified in the project plan, manages day-to-day activities, generates regular status reports, conducts regular status meetings, manages the change control process, coordinates contact with all other vendors, and ensures the project's timely and successful completion.

❏ **Data Modeler**: The data modeler creates the subject area diagram, logical data model, and data warehouse data model, as well as conducts discussions with key business analysts and end-users to identify requirements and data sources.

❏ Select group of **end-users and business analysts**: This group works with the data modeler to identify data model data sources and requirements. These groups' participation will ensure that the highest return on the data warehouse investment is delivered to your business.

Table 3–1 shows how the relationship between the end-users and data warehouse project team works.

Table 3–1 End-user and Project Team Relationship

Business End-users	Data Warehouse Project Team
Identify strategic data	Develops the data model
Define data archive requirements	Provides data archiving and retrieval
Approve data source	Identifies data source
Determine level of granularity	Does extracts, transformations, and loads
Identify data integrity issues	Identifies data integrity issues
Define DSS applications	Develops DSS applications
Train the end-users	Trains the trainers
Define the data	Documents the data

Each of these groups plays a pivotal role in each phase of the warehouse project, including development, implementation, and maintenance. *And, because a data warehouse is never finished, these roles do not stop and start. They continue throughout the life of the warehouse.* The cross-functional implementation team fosters a vision for the organization rather than a focus on a particular business area.

Readiness Assessment

Because data warehousing is still new, conducting an orientation (or readiness assessment) is critical. A readiness assessment typically includes discussions with the executive sponsor, potential team members, and end-users to ascertain their level of understanding of data warehouses in general. The goal is to identify the organization's preparedness (or gaps in knowledge) to develop and deploy the data warehouse. Consider writing a readiness assessment, including technology, data, and education issues that address specific project risk and success factors.

> Consider issuing a project readiness assessment report prior to project deployment. This step results in a level of confidence that the investment in the implemented solution can meet expectations and requirements. The project readiness report:
>
> • Lowers the risk of big surprises during implementation
> • Provides a proactive approach to problem resolution
> • Assesses corporate commitment
> • Re-identifies project size and scope
> • Identifies critical success factors
> • Provides a review of the plan, team skills, and tools selected for the solution

When conducting the readiness assessment, your goal is to determine specific training needs. For example: Do end-users need two days of orientation? Does the DBA need three days of training? If you determine your group needs orientation or educational materials, encourage them to review Section 1 of this book.

When interviewing the **end-users**, determine: What are they expecting from the data warehouse? What do they think it will change about their jobs? What data/information will now be more accessible? Focus on strategic decisions (versus tactical) with end users—they should understand that instead of requesting reports from the information technology group, they will be expected to generate their own reports. And, response times will be slower than the typical OLTP system response times.

On the other hand, when interviewing the **DBA**, ascertain: What is his/her level of knowledge of a star schema? What about techniques for increasing performance? Does he/she know how to use EXPLAIN plans to tune SQL queries? How current is he/she on parallel technologies? Does he/she stay up-to-date on the latest bitmapped indexing and star optimizer technologies?

Finally, when interviewing the **data modeler**, find out: What experience does he/she have interviewing subject matter experts to gather requirements? What data modeling tools is he/she familiar with?

Determining the Initial Business Requirements

The project sponsor, business analysts, and project manager are responsible for identifying and defining the purpose of the data warehouse, ensuring that the warehouse meets the strategic objectives of the business. Data warehousing experts agree on one thing: If you don't know what and who you're building the warehouse for, the project is doomed. A significant portion of time is spent determining the appropriate data elements to be propagated to the data warehouse. One client took two to three months to uncover the data elements, definitions, and business rules maintained in each of its operational systems. It is critical to allocate some percentage of time in the data planning phase to determine common data definitions and business rules. As such, you should be able to comprehensively answer the following questions before beginning the actual implementation of the data warehouse. In other words, *you should understand the business problem you're trying to solve by implementing the data warehouse.*

1. What are the most critical business questions you need to answer as part of your job?
2. How do you respond to these questions?
3. What is the mission of your area, department, and/or organization?
   - Is your group or area of responsibility meeting its sales goals?
   - If so (or not), by what percentage?
   - Is that percentage increasing or decreasing?
4. How do you deliver on this mission?

5. Where is your control repository of data?

6. What data do you need to access to successfully carry out your job?

7. Are there specific targets, forecasts, or actual sales you use or monitor as part of your job?

8. How much historical data do you need to answer key business questions?

9. What information inaccessible in the past would be valuable to you?

Additionally, do some initial analysis on the directive of the data warehouse. Ask your team:

1. Why is the data warehouse project being undertaken?

2. What are the overall goals and objectives of the data warehouse?

3. What is supposed to be accomplished with the data warehouse?

4. Is there an overall strategic vision for the data warehouse?

You can discuss these issues via a group gathering, where you publicly assess the project. Communicate a clearly defined goal for the meeting, have a structured agenda, engage an unbiased facilitator, provide information in advance so attendees are prepared, allocate enough time to ensure that the goals of the meeting are met, and assign someone to take minutes. Participants should include the project manager, subject matter experts, business analysts, data modeler, and key end-users.

Organizing the Project Plan and Scope

The project definition and scope document functions as the data warehouse's implementation business plan. The document describes the project and identifies the objectives, critical success factors, assumptions, and issues. Most importantly, the project definition and scope document sets expectations up-front as to what each phase of the data warehouse deployment will include. The scope document is not meant to be all-encompassing, but it should be thorough enough that the end-users and sponsors of the project have their expectations set appropriately. (Note that the scope document will initially identify the pilot deployment.)

An example project scope document follows. You can easily modify this example to meet your planning needs.

Project Scope Document

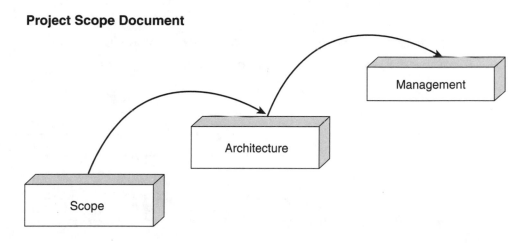

Scope

- Project Definition
  (For example, a retailer we worked with defined the scope of its data warehouse as product narrowing and product movement. Another retailer we worked with implemented a data warehouse to do market basket analysis.)

  _____
  _____
  _____
  _____
  _____
  _____

- Subject Area Focus
  (For example, our retailer focused on inventory and product.)

  _____
  _____
  _____
  _____
  _____
  _____

- Specific Goals of the Project

  (For example, our retailer's goal was to stock only products that would sell and to eliminate any that didn't have broad market appeal.)

  _____

  _____

  _____

  _____

  _____

  _____

- Team Members/Roles

  (For example, a data warehouse architect to roll out and mange the new hardware infrastructure; a data modeler to create a way of uniformly depicting data; and, an end-user to test the end-user access tool.)

  _____

  _____

  _____

  _____

  _____

  _____

- Other Required Resources

  (For example, what other information technology or business support organizations are required for the data warehouse deployment, training, and management? Do you need a UNIX system administrator?)

  _____

  _____

  _____

  _____

  _____

- Critical Success Factors

  (For example, our retailer's critical success factors included increasing prod-uct profitability, increasing the business analyst's and end-user's decision-making abilities; and reducing the cost of hard copy distributed reports.)

  _____

  _____

  _____

  _____

  _____

- Measurements of Success

  (For example, initial measurements of success determined by our retailer included increasing end-user interaction with the data warehouse by 50% while simultaneously identifying and eliminating 60% of the non-moving inventory.)

  _____

  _____

  _____

  _____

  _____

Infrastructure

- Physical Architecture (hardware, software, end user tools)

  (See Chapter 4 for a comprehensive discussion of architectural components.)

  _____

  _____

  _____

  _____

  _____

- Data Warehouse Source(s)
  (For example, our retailer's sales data came directly from the point of sale, OLTP system; the inventory listing and stores by geographic location came from the mainframe system.)

  _____
  _____
  _____
  _____
  _____

- Samples of Appropriate Queries
  (For example, include screen captures from your end-user tool depicting the standard slice-and-dice and/or collaboration query built for your analysts.)

Management

- Methodology and Approach
  (Make us proud. State here that you'll be following the methodology identified in this book........)

  _____
  _____
  _____
  _____
  _____

- End-user Requirements (or your strategy for capturing these requirements)
  (Use the sample questions included at the end of this chapter to help capture the end user requirements.)

  _____
  _____
  _____
  _____
  _____

- Project Costs—Benefits, ROI?

  (For example, identify staff resources and their associated costs for a three-month time period; identify the initial hardware and software purchase costs; identify the ongoing hardware and software maintenance costs; and, identify the costs of any training or education.)

  _____

  _____

  _____

  _____

  _____

- Project Schedule

  (See the sample project plan included in this chapter—and insert your completed project plan here.)

- Project Issues, Risks, and Expectations

  (For example, is management allotting the appropriate amount of time to design and deploy the warehouse? Do you have appropriately skilled staff? What integration issues with legacy systems are you expecting?)

Building the Project Plan

The project plan details the design and construction of the data warehouse. The plan consists of tasks for building the data warehouse, the time frame for each activity, deliverables, milestones, assigned resources, and costs. We used Microsoft Project to build the included project plan.

The project manager uses a project management tool to develop a project plan and track the progress of a project. Microsoft Project is a tool you can use to develop a plan, track progress over time, identify critical paths, estimate completion, and replan due to changes. Using a structured planning tool to support your project ensures that you have a mechanism for developing and tracking plans, as well as providing a consistent platform that enables your group to share project plans from a consistent starting point through the use of project files. Using a project management tool also gives teams the ability to automatically trigger task notices to project participants and to receive project task updates in a consistent, automated way. Use the tool to archive project information, particularly as a project moves from one phase to the next. Updates to all status information can be automatically filed and traced to their source.

Specifically, Microsoft Project:

- Allows users to create and edit projects, specify resources, lay out task types and durations, define integrated sub-projects, and build top-down hierarchies and task-dependency relations
- Links multiple projects for cross-leveling and performs "what if" analyses
- Has graphics and reporting tools that generate customized Gantt, PERT, WBS, and Cost/Resource charts for specific audiences and applications with WYSIWYG, on-screen, interactive graphics capabilities
- Outputs to a wide range of devices, including plotters

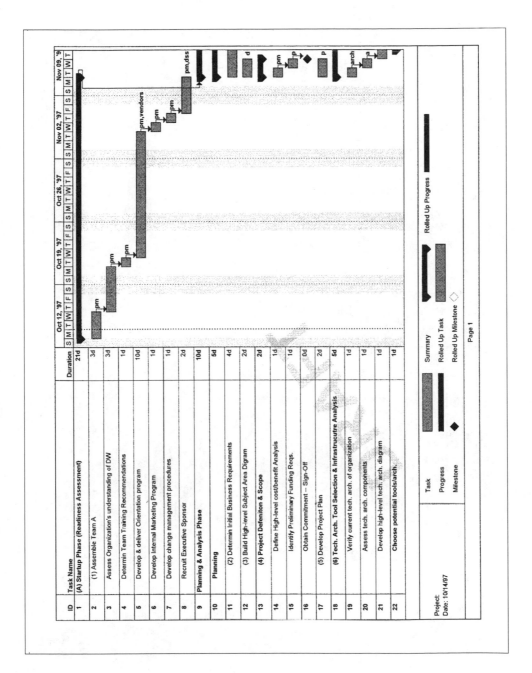

ID	Task Name	Duration
1	(A) Startup Phase (Readiness Assessment)	21d
2	(1) Assemble Team A	3d
3	Assess Organization's understanding of DW	3d
4	Determin Team Training Recommendations	1d
5	Develop & deliver Orientation program	10d
6	Develop Internal Marketing Program	1d
7	Develop change management procedures	1d
8	Recruit Executive Sponsor	2d
9	Planning & Analysis Phase	10d
10	Planning	5d
11	(2) Determin Initial Business Requirements	4d
12	(3) Build High-level Subject Area Digram	2d
13	(4) Project Defeniton & Scope	2d
14	Define High-level cost/benefit Analysis	1d
15	Identify Prelinninary Funding Reqs.	1d
16	Obtain Commitment -- Sign-Off	0d
17	(5) Develop Project Plan	2d
18	(6) Tech. Arch. Tool Selection & Infrastrucutre Analysis.	5d
19	Verify current tech. arch. of organization	1d
20	Assess tech. arch. components	1d
21	Develop high-level tech. arch. diagram	1d
22	Choose potential tools/arch.	1d

Project:
Date: 10/14/97

Task		Summary
Progress		Rolled Up Task
Milestone	◆	Rolled Up Milestone ◇
		Rolled Up Progress

Page 1

ID	Task Name	Duration
23	select scalable hw,os,storage	1d
24	select parallel dbms	1d
25	select CASE data modeling tool	1d
26	select extraction/load tool	1d
27	select metadata tool	1d
28	select end user access tool(s)	1d
29	Estimate costs of recommended arch.	1d
30	Deliver Detailed Scope Doc & get Sign-off	1d
31	(7) Assemble Team B	4d
32	Train Team on tools	5d
33	Analysis	10d
34	(8) Gather Additional subject area reqs.	6d
35	Create detailed reqs. work sheet	1d
36	Interview SMEs of Legacy Syst.	1d
37	Interview Key End Users	1d
38	Determin Functional Reqs	1d
39	Determin End User Data Access Reqs.	1d
40	Define Preliminary Acceptance Critera	1d
41	(9) Source System identification	4d
42	Compile information on candidate sources	1d
43	Assess characteristics of candidate sources	1d
44	Interview SMEs of Legacy Syst.	1d

Project:
Date: 10/14/97

Task		Summary		Rolled Up Progress
Progress		Rolled Up Task		
Milestone		Rolled Up Milestone		

Page 2

ID	Task Name	Duration
45	Develop recommendation for source system	1d
46	Compile source target mappings	1d
47	(10) Logical Data Warehouse Data Model	10d
48	Review OLTP logical data models	1d
49	Create logical Automic level data model	4d
50	Create dw logical data model	4d
51	Determin meta data requirements	1d
52	(11) Conduct Sizing estimates	6d
53	Data Volunme	3d
54	Processor requirements	3d
55	Develop/Deliver Detailed Scope Document-Sign-off	1d
56	Design Phase	4d
57	Install configure Development Environment	1d
58	Intall H/W, OS. SW tools, DBMS on Server	1d
59	Intall H/W, OS. SW tools, on client	1d
60	Ensure Network Connectivity	1d
61	Order Production Environment HW	1d
62	(12) Create Automic level Physical Model	3d
63	Create Sum. Dept. Level Physical Model	3d
64	Determin/Design backup & mirror requirements	2d
65	Design Purge Process	1d
66	(14a) Design extraction	1d

Project:
Date: 10/14/97

Task		Summary		Rolled Up Progress
Progress		Rolled Up Task		
Milestone	◆	Rolled Up Milestone	◇	

Page 3

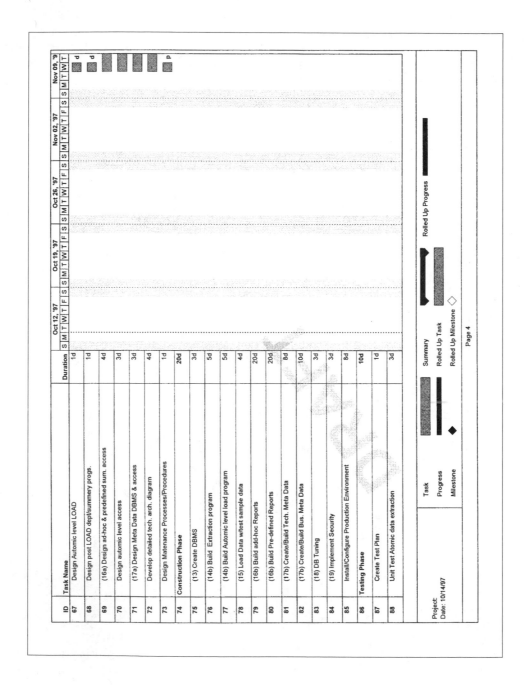

ID	Task Name	Duration	Oct 12, '97	Oct 19, '97	Oct 26, '97	Nov 02, '97	Nov 09, '9
67	Design Automic level LOAD	1d					d
68	Design post LOAD dept/summery progs.	1d					d
69	(16a) Design ad-hoc & predefined sum. access	4d					
70	Design automic level access	3d					
71	(17a) Design Meta Data DBMS & access	3d					
72	Develop detailed tech. arch. diagram	4d					
73	Design Matenance Processes/Procedures	1d					
74	Construction Phase	20d					p
75	(13) Create DBMS	3d					
76	(14b) Build Extraction program	5d					
77	(14b) Build Automic level load program	5d					
78	(15) Load Data w/test sample data	4d					
79	(16b) Build add-hoc Reports	20d					
80	(16b) Build Pre-defined Reports	20d					
81	(17b) Create/Build Tech. Meta Data	8d					
82	(17b) Create/Build Bus. Meta Data	10d					
83	(18) DB Tuning	3d					
84	(19) Implement Security	3d					
85	Install/Configure Production Environment	8d					
86	Testing Phase	10d					
87	Create Test Plan	1d					
88	Unit Test Atomic data extraction	3d					

Project:
Date: 10/14/97

Task		Summary		Rolled Up Progress
Progress		Rolled Up Task		
Milestone	◆	Rolled Up Milestone	◇	

Page 4

ID	Task Name	Duration	Oct 12, '97	Oct 19, '97	Oct 26, '97	Nov 02, '97	Nov 09, '97
89	Unit Test Automic data transformation & loading	3d					
90	System test integration	2d					
91	Unit Test Automic post load sum.	5d					
92	Test data warehouse maintenace process	4d					
93	Unit test Each Report & validate each measure	10d					
94	System Test data validataion	5d					
95	Conduct Data Quality Review	4d					
96	System test dw activity monitor procedures	3d					
97	System test archive and restore procedures	4d					
98	System test security	3d					
99	Conduct Regression Test	5d					
100	End User Acceptance Testing	8d					
101	User Sign-Off	0d					
102	UPDATE data as needed during test cycle	1d					
103	(21) Training	10d					
104	Implementaion Phase	10d					
105	Place data extraction into production	1d					
106	Place atomic data transform & load into production	1d					
107	Place post automic sum. into produciton	1d					
108	Place dw maintenace process into produciton	1d					
109	FULLY Populate current subject area (load history)	10d					
110	(18) Performance Tuning again - on-going	2d					

Project:
Date: 10/14/97

Task	Summary	Rolled Up Progress
Progress	Rolled Up Task	
Milestone	Rolled Up Milestone	

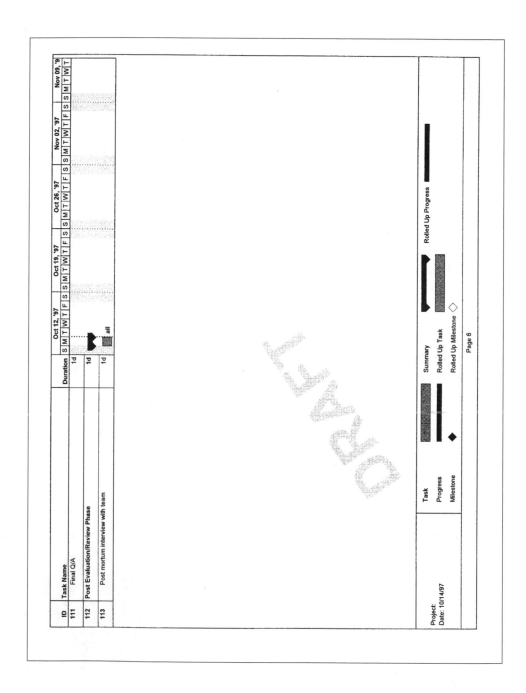

ID	Task Name	Duration
111	Final Q/A	1d
112	**Post Evaluation/Review Phase**	1d
113	Post mortum interview with team	1d

Project:
Date: 10/14/97

Task		Summary		Rolled Up Progress	
Progress		Rolled Up Task			
Milestone	◆	Rolled Up Milestone	◇		

Page 6

Assembling the Support Team

Resources from network services, operations, database administration, and application systems help define the initial technical architecture and play an active role in expansion, maintenance, and support of the warehouse. Along with the initial team members identified earlier in the chapter, the data warehouse team should consist of the following resources (Figure 3–2):

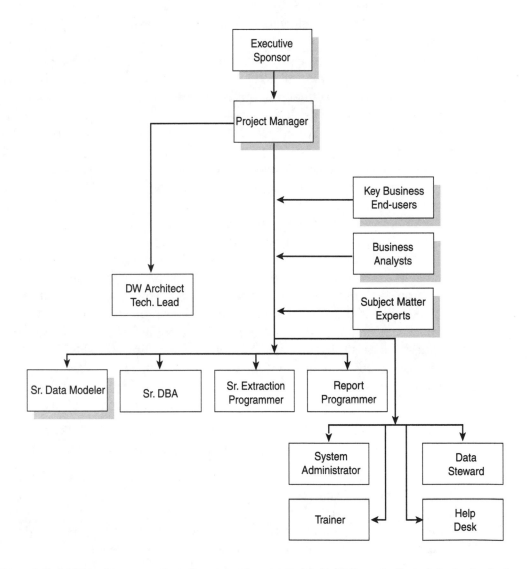

Figure 3–2 Additional team members (team members assembled initially are indicated via shadowing).

Technical staff members work closely with the architecture staff to plan, design, and implement data extraction and transformation. With data elements for a subject area often spread among multiple data sources, the integration of data from multiple, disparate data sources is a complex process and requires a clear understanding of the sources and methodology to perform integration. Technical staff includes:

❑ **Data Warehouse Architect**: Concentrates on the architecture and infrastructure aspects of the project, with the flexibility and extensibility of the data warehouse as the primary goals. The data warehouse architect assists in conducting readiness assessments, creating management procedures, planning, and implementing the infrastructure. After gathering requirements, the technical and data architectural support requirements must be defined. Data collection rates, volumes, and timing from every point in the warehouse dictate network capacity, transfer rates, storage volumes, and growth rate of the warehouse.

❑ **Database Administrator**: Creates the physical database schema, manages performance, creates sizing estimates, performs backups, assists with loads, and implements security.

❑ **Programmer/Analyst:** Creates extraction/transformation programs.

❑ **Business Analyst**: Knowledgeable in the needs and requirements of end-users. Documents end-user requirements and maintains business measurement descriptions. Business analysts provide valuable knowledge and guidance from both the user's and business' perspectives, bringing a positive relationship with the business departments to the project. Analysts can assist with the preparation and transformation of corporate operational data into business analysis-oriented data, in addition to assisting with the reconciliation of warehouse data and historical data.

❑ **Report Programmer**: Leads the installation, implementation, and demonstration of the end-user tool and creates standard query templates as identified in the requirements analysis.

Additional support staff involved in the data warehouse project will include:

❑ **Systems Administration Technical Support**: Sets up the technical environment, installs hardware, operating system, storage devices, and networks, and maintains the operations of the system.

❑ **Trainer**: Creates the training curriculum and trains the end-users.

❑ **Help Desk**: Supports the end-users in accessing the warehouse.

End-user staff will include:

☐ **Subject Matter Expert**: Facilitates the extraction process, including extraction scheduling.

☐ **Data Stewards**: Resolve data integration issues, determine data security, document data definitions, calculations, and summarizations, and maintain and update business rules. Power end-users who understand the data and the information it provides may assume these roles.

Assembling Additional Business Requirements

This step differs from the initial requirements gathering because it is subject area-specific. For example, you would ask your sales organization: Where is information stored? Which is the system of record? What information do you want via reports? What are your power users', casual users', and end-users' expectations? Do you want daily transaction reports or weekly transaction reports?

During this phase, you'll interview end users extensively, as well as gather information about the source systems that will be used to populate the warehouse. Interviewing the end-users is critical because they give the designer insight into the needs and expectations of the business user community and allow the designer to set expectations. When meeting with end-users, ensure a positive exchange of information by setting an agenda, establishing who the participants will be, reviewing all relevant materials, gaining consensus on the scope, goals and purpose of the session, managing the logistics of the session, and educating participants as to what their contributions will be. The ideal sessions are one hour in length with two to four data warehouse team members, the subject area manager, and several of his/her subordinates (for example, the Central Region Sales Manager and several of his/her salespersons).

Interview key business end-users to identify and/or clarify their requirements for the current implementation. The business requirements analysts should document these requirements to identify the measures used (such as gross profit percent, units, or amounts). Interview the subject matter experts to identify how these measures are derived or calculated. Your goal is to capture more detailed requirements than those identified in the Planning & Analysis Phase. The results of the end-user interviews aid in defining the final scope of the effort, identifying critical data required by the business, and facilitating project planning. The results of this process should include:

- A prioritized set of business measures
- The business definitions of these measures
- The components that make up these measures
- The definitions of each component

During these interviews, the end-users should prioritize their requirements for information. Also, be sure to resolve conflicting definitions for similar or common business terms—most importantly, identify:

- Each end-user's most important business requirements
- The amount of historical information required to support those requirements
- The relationships between categories and types of data required
- A time to re-interview end-users to validate the discussed requirements

Next, the business analyst identifies additional functionality considerations for current or future implementations, including archiving of data, restoring archived data, monitoring data acquisition or data access, securing the data warehouse, and distributing the data. This is accomplished during the interview process by gathering information related to:

- The need for access to historical data
- The response time expectations for historical data
- The frequency of historical data access
- The confidentiality of the data

Formal documentation of the acceptance criteria is key to establishing common, achievable expectations. These expectations should include:

- Types of questions to be answered by the data warehouse
- Amount of training required for the end-users
- Response time for the average query
- Ease of use of the data access environment
- Data correctness
- Data completeness
- Frequency of data updates

These expectations define a set of objectives for the data warehouse project team to use throughout the development, construction, and testing processes. These criteria serve as the basis for developing the user acceptance test plan. Presenting acceptance criteria in a formalized manner helps end-users to acknowledge whether they would perceive the data warehouse as successful if these needs were not satisfied.

What Am I Trying to Find Out?

Questions you can ask during the fact-finding interviews include both general business questions and technical specifics, such as current data repository and reporting requirements. This step differs from the initial requirements gathering because it is subject area-specific. We've included some "starter" questions below and grouped them into subject area categories.

How Do You Do Your Job?

(Goal: Determine day-to-day business requirements.)

1. What is your department's or organization's business mission?
2. How does each department member accomplish this mission?
3. What deliverables are required from each department member?
4. What information is needed to meet these deliverables?
5. Where is this information currently stored?
6. How do you access the information?
7. How is the data used (ad hoc, reports)?
8. What future uses of the data do you anticipate?
9. What are your specific business measures (for example: units sold, unit cost, unit retail, unit gross profit, unit net gross profit minus adjustments, percent discounts, percent difference versus last year)?
10. Do you want to keep revenue by salesperson or other dimensions, including product, location, month, year, and/or customer?
11. List any other specifics you monitor as part of your job (for example: customer count, units sold).

What is the Focus of Your Organization?

(Goal: Get specific!)

Common answers include: *to be more customer focused . . . to be more quality driven. . . .* If your participants answer, "To be more customer focused," you could then ask:

1. What do you mean by *customer focused*?
2. How do you think about customers?
3. How many customers do you have?
4. How do you group customers? Do these groupings change dynamically?

How Do You Contribute to the Company's Revenue?
(Goal: What information is critical to this group's success?)

1. For which part of the business can you measure profit?
2. What are the components of revenue and cost that make up profit?
3. Are the components accurately measured? Do you need to see more granular levels of the data?
4. How do you track quality measures on product deliveries? Is that in a separate system?
5. What do your competitors do that you don't?
6. Do you want to do that also?
7. How do you measure success in your group?

What Does Your Data Need to Look Like?
(Goal: What granularity of data do the end-users need?)

1. Do you need to see the data at a daily grain?
2. Do you need to distinguish Tuesdays from Saturdays?
3. Do you need to see how promoted items get depleted on a day-to-day basis?
4. Are monthly snapshots sufficient?
5. Do you need to track products at the UPC level?
6. Do you want to track sales at the individual store level? Customer level?
7. Do you want to track sales at an individual promotion level in a store on a particular day? How many promotions are there per year? What is a promotion? What is a special?

Or, if a transaction-level view is necessary, ask the following:
1. How many transaction types are there?
2. How many of these have associated reason codes?
3. Which ones are interesting to the business?
4. Do you want to break down the activity by transaction type and reason code?
5. Do you look at counts of particular transaction types?
6. Do you look at the timings of certain kinds of transactions?
7. Would you want to ask how many of the orders were taken on the phone?
8. How is the weekly or monthly revenue calculated?

What Else Would Make You a More Effective Employee?
(Goal: What are the end-user expectations of the data warehouse?)

1. Do you expect this database to tie to the general ledger each month?

2. Do you maintain a special store profile for descriptions?

3. Do you maintain customer behavior scores of credit scores or do you maintain ranking versus scores?

4. Do you have access to the original credit applications made by customers?

5. Would it make sense to associate demographic data with stores or sales regions?

6. Does someone in marketing already have such demographic data?

7. Do you have a table of ingredients for each product?

8. Who else do you think would be interested in this data? Are they your clients or vice versa?

9. What happens when you change the organization's geography hierarchy?

10. How soon after the end of the day do you need the data to be available?

By the Way...

- Push back on *scope creep*:
  Scope creep occurs when new requirements are added throughout the project life cycle. Your job is to deliver: 1) a data warehouse built to reflect the initial business requirements; 2) in the projected time frame; 3) to the end-users. Add additional requirements determined during the project to the next iteration. Unfortunately, a client of mine accepted requirements throughout the life cycle of the project and lengthened the data warehouse implementation from four months to one year. As a result, data warehousing end-users didn't see the value of the data warehouse project for an entire year.

- Set user expectations pertaining to *response time* up-front:
  If end-users expect sub-second response times, they're going to be pretty disappointed when they start receiving sub-minute or even sub-hour response times. Communicate the correlation between data warehouse data volume and response time.

- Manage detail data in the enterprise data warehouse by:
  Remembering your data warehouse architecture and by storing detail data for data mining and for building departmental data marts in the enterprise data warehouse. Don't get rushed and store detailed data in a data mart. Your OLAP tools will **not** be able to analyze that data.

- Enable end-user access to the data warehouse as quickly as possible by:
  Setting up a feedback loop for understanding and incorporating changes and suggestions and by resolving issues. Use this forum for determining requirements for the additional iterations of the data warehouse.

- Make end-user access as easy as possible:
  The choice of the meta data tool is critical for data warehouse navigation and data retrieval. Ease-of-use benefits are obvious.

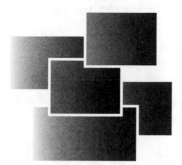

Chapter 4

CHOOSE YOUR WEAPONS

Choosing the components that comprise a data warehouse is difficult. You must consider, among others factors, ease of use, performance, cost, and vendor stability. Human factors also affect the decision—products are frequently chosen according to corporate politics (the golf course is frequently applauded for closing a deal). The product positioning swirl and aggressive vendor posturing result in organizations constantly changing their views about the strengths and weaknesses of technologies. And, those with purchasing power are bombarded with product information, briefing requests, and invitations for a few rounds of golf.

Choosing the components of a data warehouse involves more than select-

What was the task at hand again? Oh yeah, matching your organization's needs to the capabilities of the products.

ing a DBMS or choosing an end-user access tool. Rather, it's a process that requires the following: first of all, data warehouse analysis, definition, and design; second, data acquisition (extraction, transformation, and scrubbing); third, data warehouse management; fourth, creation of the meta data information directory; fifth, enabling data access; and finally, implementing the network middleware.

The data warehouse, or more descriptively, the decision support system (DSS), includes a broad range of functions and user types. User types include the novice end-user, application developer, business analyst, and the executive. DSS tools must account for this broad range of users and each user's unique requirements. They must also provide a scalable solution for a broad range of uses, including executive information systems, multimedia, and specialized scientific and statistical analysis tools. Data warehousing and the creation of informational databases to move decision support activities off of operational systems is improving the decision support process. Middleware within the warehouse that moves and enhances the data provides a greater ability for the end-user to more easily access the data. The introduction of meta data (data about data) and information catalog-type tools allows the end-user to more easily find and understand the data. Querying informational databases also allows you to open decision support to a broader audience due to less concern for impact on the operational systems and by providing rationalized data organized for analysis.

High-end decision support, processing hundreds of gigabytes or terabytes of data, is becoming more and more important as the data explosion continues. It is one of the driving factors for parallel processing requirements. This chapter provides information you need to respond to the need for more and faster and better answers from data. We first position data warehouses and data marts and then discuss the merits and/or drawbacks of MOLAP and ROLAP. Next we look at single-solution providers versus multiple vendors. To help you build your solution, we discuss database storage vendors and products, end-user tools, hardware platforms, storage subsystems, extraction, transformation, and scrubbing tools, meta data tools, and data modeling tools.

Let's first determine if your organization's requirements can be met by a data warehouse or data mart and then discuss the appropriate infrastructure. To ensure that you don't fall short, review Figure 4–1 to verify that your solution reflects all of the data warehousing components. Consider using the following sample form (Figure 4–2) to get an idea of your progress.

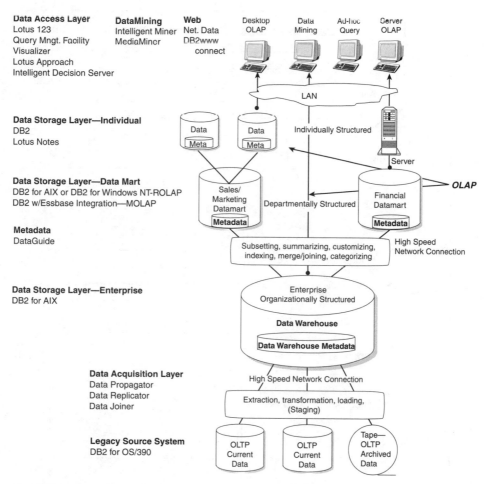

Data Access Layer
Lotus 123
Query Mngt. Facility
Visualizer
Lotus Approach
Intelligent Decision Server

DataMining
Intelligent Miner
MediaMiner

Web
Net. Data
DB2www
connect

Desktop OLAP

Data Mining

Ad-hoc Query

Server OLAP

LAN

Data Storage Layer—Individual
DB2
Lotus Notes

Data
Meta

Data
Meta

Individually Structured

Server

Data Storage Layer—Data Mart
DB2 for AIX or DB2 for Windows NT-ROLAP
DB2 w/Essbase Integration—MOLAP

Sales/
Marketing
Datamart
Metadata

Departmentally Structured

Financial
Datamart
Metadata

OLAP

Metadata
DataGuide

Subsetting, summarizing, customizing, indexing, merge/joining, categorizing

High Speed
Network Connection

Data Storage Layer—Enterprise
DB2 for AIX

Enterprise
Organizationally Structured

Data Warehouse

Data Warehouse Metadata

Data Acquisition Layer
Data Propagator
Data Replicator
Data Joiner

High Speed Network Connection

Extraction, transformation, loading,
(Staging)

Legacy Source System
DB2 for OS/390

OLTP
Current
Data

OLTP
Current
Data

Tape—
OLTP
Archived
Data

Other IBM Infrastructure Components
Hardware: RS/6000 with AIX
Hardware Storage: Seascape—IBM 7133 Storage Subsystem; Megastar MP 3575 Tape Library; ADSM Archive Software
Networking: Routers, Hubs, Switches, Adapter Cards, Cables, Monitoring Software (Tivoli TME 10 NetView)

Misc. Software
Administration: DBA—DB2 Visual Explain, DB2 Estimator, DataHub for UNIX, DB2 Enterprise Control Center
Administration: OS—Tivoli TME 10, Nways Manager
Data Modeling: TeamConnection DataAtlas
Data Warehouse: Visual Warehouse

Figure 4–1 IBM's data warehousing solution.

Data Warehouse Component Checklist

Component   [   ]

Product Name   [   ]

Vendor Name   [   ]

Dependencies   [   ]

Status

                        Ordered on Date   [   ]

                   Scheduled Delivery Data   [   ]

        Scheduled Installation Time Frame   [   ]

            Implementation Personnel   [   ]

            Configuration Specifications [   ]

                        Comments   [   ]

Figure 4–2 Sample information-gathering form.

This chapter's deliverable will be a detailed architectural design of your data warehouse. And although we'll discuss the key players in the server, front-end tool, and database spaces, our intention is not to provide comprehensive descriptions of all products in every category, but rather to highlight the strengths and weaknesses of representative products. Don't make any purchasing decision without studying trade magazines such as *Database Advisor*, *Database Programming and Design*, *Datamation*, and *DBMS Magazine*, as well as visiting vendors' Web sites to obtain more details on commercial products, white papers, and case studies. Check out the Data Warehousing Information Center for references on data warehousing and OLAP (http://pwp.starnet-inc.com/larryg/index.html).

Before choosing your data warehouse components, review candidate products that support both the current implementation of the data warehouse and the long-term direction:

✔ Identify the components for the current implementation (including operating systems, hardware/servers, RDBMS, MDD, DSSs, networking, and support for each).

✔ Ensure component integration. Remember hardware (data warehouse enterprise platform, the departmental platform, and the desktop), software (RDBMS, operating system, data cleansing, data transport, data extraction, data summarization, process scheduling, data sorting, meta data management, data warehouse monitoring, data modeling, security, and data access—analysis, connectivity/networking, and backup/restore), and networking (telecommunication lines, LAN, WAN, bridge, router, switch, gateway, modem, Web server, and software (TCP/IP)). Based on the product features, ensure that no incompatibilities exist.

✔ Estimate costs and obtain approval (evaluate the requirements against the products to ensure that capacity and volume can be satisfied).

Before diving into our discussions of data modeling/CASE tools, hardware and storage, DBMS, end-user tools, and meta data tools, let's first take a look at several implementation issues:

- The enterprise data warehouse versus the data mart
- MOLAP versus ROLAP
- Total solution providers versus multiple product vendors

Which Way to Go?

Data Warehouse or Data Mart?

When designing and constructing the data warehouse, companies can either: 1) establish an enterprisewide architecture and then construct data warehouses or data marts which conform to the enterprisewide architecture; or 2) implement a highly-focused and targeted data mart project aimed at a specific area of the business. The disparities in enterprise systems started theorists envisioning data warehouses—online repositories of scrubbed, detailed, and summarized enterprise data based on common business measures serving the needs of business users, promoting accurate reporting, and off-loading the query processing overhead from transaction systems. These repositories would:

- Share common business assumptions
- Protect the enterprise from inconsistent reporting across business units
- Deliver access to detailed corporate data via a mix of quick-response summaries and aggregates
- Lessen the expense required to create and modify legacy transformation feeds into multiple decision support engines
- Reduce the daily burden on wide area networks (WANs)
- Scale to meet the needs of the enterprise

Embracing this enterprise approach yields the best long-term results, but invokes the most angst. It is difficult, expensive, and time-consuming to achieve consensus on a single, consistent, accepted, and valid view of the business and the data it needs. Starting with smaller, more focused applications of the warehouse avoids the stress of the enterprise approach by limiting the extent of the implementation. It's also simpler architecturally—there are usually limited data sets and limited user views. Basically, the more focused approach trades the near term pain of dealing with data standardization issues for the longer term pain of dealing with cross-organization operational issues. In this approach, each department is responsible for extracting whatever data it needs, defining its own meta data, and using its own private warehouses for decision support at the departmental level. Obviously: 1) this architecture is difficult to evolve to an enterprise view; and 2) the lack of data standardization prevents analysts in one organization from accessing information from another organization's warehouse which might be of use to them in their analyses. Each mart can create confusion, overlapping, and contradictory views of the business like: What is a customer? A product? A sale?

> The data that resides in the data warehouse is granular, while the data in the data mart is refined.

Understanding Data Marts

What is the appeal of the data mart? Well, as data warehouses grow, more and more departmental DSS processing is done inside the data warehouse, leading to resource consumption. If a department has its own data mart, it can customize the data as the data flows into the data mart from the data warehouse. The department can summarize, sort, select, and structure its own data without considering other departments. And typically, the department can select a smaller amount of historical data than that found in the data warehouse. Finally, the processing and storage costs on a data mart server are significantly less than the unit cost for the machine that houses the data warehouse. Unlike physically centralized data warehouses, which typically expand between 3-5 times every 18 months, the data mart generally expands horizontally, breeding requests for more data marts at brush-fire speed. The data mart is a powerful and natural extension of the data warehouse because it extends DSS to the departmental environment.

The more focused data mart is preferable in organizations that have a business problem with a single focus that requires data existing in only a few places. The user of the data mart environment is sometimes called the departmental decision support system (DSS) analyst—an individual who does decision-making with a departmental bias. The departmental DSS analyst is not a technician, but rather a business person making mid- to long-term, strategic decisions.

Note that performance expectations in the DSS environment are entirely different from those in the OLTP environment. For example, DSS environment response time requirements vary from one minute to 24 hours. The issue of performance is relaxed because of the abundance of data and the high levels of data exploration. In turn, performance in the data mart is somewhat different from the data warehouse because: 1) the data mart is used by regular users who have predictable data requirements (enabling reasonable performance objectives to be set); and 2) there is less data in the data mart environment. Optimal performance in the data mart is achieved by:

- Making extensive use of indexes
- Using star joins
- Limiting the volume of data that is found in the data mart
- Creating arrays of data
- Creating aggregate records
- Creating pre-joined tables

> A **regular** user undertakes standard, repetitive queries on small units of data that usually have predictable responses. A **power** user does random ad hoc queries, generating unpredictable responses on large units of data. Most users are **regular**. Note that front end tool functionality and pricing are structured along these user definitions as well.

Data is loaded into the data mart from the data warehouse via a load program that takes into consideration:

- Loading schedule and speed
- How frequently the program is run
- Total or partial refreshment
- Data customization
- Selecting, re-sequencing, merging, and aggregating of data
- Data summarization
- Integrity of data relationships
- Load process meta data creation

The data mart environment requires data usage and data content tracking. The data usage tracker identifies:

- Data being accessed
- Active users
- Average response time
- Amount of data being requested
- Busiest times of the day, week, and month
- If aggregate tables need to be built and where

The data content tracker looks at data mart content, data integrity, growth rate, and data access.

What If?

If:

a. You require write access for *What if?* analysis

b. Your data is under 50GB

c. Your timetable to implement is 60–90 days

d. You don't have a DBA or data modeler personnel

e. You're developing a general-purpose application for inventory movement or assets management

Then:

Consider an MDD solution for your data mart (we review Oracle Express, Arbor's Essbase, and Pilot's Lightship later in this chapter).

If:

a. Your data is over 100GB

b. You have a "read-only" requirement

Then:

Consider an RDBMS for the data mart. If you're using an SMP hardware platform, review the strengths and weaknesses analysis of Oracle, Red Brick, DB2, Informix, and Sybase that follows later in this chapter.

If:

a. Your data is over 1TB

b. Your hardware platform is MPP

Then:

DB2 is the clear winner, with Informix coming in a distant second. Oracle is a popular marketplace choice, but is poorly designed for an MPP hardware configuration. (Be on the lookout for the improvements promised in Oracle 8.)

If:

a. You're building a data mart

b. You're using an MDD

Then:

You don't need a data modeler. Rather, you need an MDD data mart application builder who will design the business model (identifying dimensions and defining business measures based on the source systems identified—see Chapter 7 for details on extraction, scrubbing, transformation, and cleansing—plus loading the data into the MDD data mart).

Prior to building separate stove pipe data marts, understand that at some point you will need to: 1) integrate and consolidate these data marts at the detailed atomic enterprise level; 2) load the MDD data marts; and 3) drill through from the data marts to the detail. Note that your data mart may outgrow the storage limitations of an MDD, creating the need for an RDBMS (in turn, requiring data modeling similar to constructing the detailed, atomic enterprise-level RDBMS).

MOLAP or ROLAP?

OLAP tools take you a step beyond query and reporting tools. Via OLAP tools, data is represented using a multidimensional model rather than the more traditional tabular data model. The traditional model defines a database schema that focuses on modeling a process or function, and the information is viewed as a set of transactions, each which occurred at some single point in time. The multidimensional model usually defines a star schema, viewing data not as a single event but rather as the cumulative effect of events over some period of time, such as weeks, then months, then years. With OLAP tools, the user generally views the data in grids or crosstabs that can be pivoted to offer different perspectives on the data. OLAP also enables interactive querying of the data. For example, a user can look at information at one aggregation (such as a sales region) and then drill down to more detailed information, such as sales by state, then city, then store.

OLAP tools do not indicate how the data is actually stored. Given that, it's not surprising that there are multiple ways to store the data, including storing the data in a dedicated multidimensional database (also referred to as MOLAP or MDD). Examples include Arbor Software's Essbase and Oracle Express Server. The other choice involves storing the data in relational databases and having an OLAP tool work directly against the data, referred to as relational OLAP (also referred to as ROLAP or RDBMS). Examples include MicroStrategy's DSS Server and related products, Informix's Informix-MetaCube, Information Advantage's Decision Suite, and Platinum Technologies' Platinum InfoBeacon. (Some also include Red Brick's Warehouse in this category, but it isn't really an OLAP tool. Rather, it is a relational database optimized for performing the types of operations that ROLAP tools need.) Table 4–1 highlights the differences between MOLAP and ROLAP.

Table 4–1 ROLAP versus MOLAP

Relational OLAP (ROLAP)	Multidimensional OLAP (MOLAP)
Scale to terabytes	Under 50GB capacity
Managing of summary tables/indexing	Instant response
Platform portability	Easier to implement
SMP and MPP	SMP only
Secure	Integrated meta data
Proven technology	
Data modeling required	

Data warehouses can be implemented on standard or extended relational DBMSs, called relational OLAP (ROLAP) servers. These servers assume that data is stored in relational databases and they support extensions to SQL and special access and implementation methods to efficiently implement the multidimensional data model and operations. In contrast, multidimensional OLAP (MOLAP) servers are servers that directly store multidimensional data in special data structures (like arrays or cubes) and implement OLAP operations over these special data structures. MOLAP servers are used for slicing and dicing numeric data in a free-form fashion (free-form within the framework of the DBMS that holds the multidimensional data). MOLAP servers have sparsely populated matrices, numeric data, and a rigid structure of data once the data enters the MOLAP DBMS framework.

Relational Databases

ROLAP servers contain both numeric and textual data, serving a much wider purpose than their MOLAP counterparts. Unlike MOLAP DBMSs (supported by specialized database management systems), ROLAP DBMSs (or RDBMSs) are supported by relational technology. RDBMSs support numeric, textual, spatial, audio, graphic, and video data, general-purpose DSS analysis, freely structured data, numerous indexes, and star schemas. ROLAP servers can have both disciplined and ad hoc usage and can contain both detailed and summarized data.

ROLAP supports large databases while enabling good performance, platform portability, exploitation of hardware advances such as parallel processing, robust security, multi-user concurrent access (including read-write with locking), recognized standards, and openness to multiple vendors' tools. ROLAP is based on familiar, proven, and already selected technologies.

ROLAP tools take advantage of parallel RDBMSs for those parts of the application processed using SQL (SQL not being a multidimensional access or processing language). So, although it is always possible to store multidimensional data in a number of relations tables (the star schema), SQL does not, by itself, support multidimensional manipulation of calculations. Therefore, ROLAP products must do these calculations either in the client software or intermediate server engine. Note, however, that Informix has integrated the ROLAP calculation engine into the RDBMS, effectively mitigating the above disadvantage.

Multidimensional Databases

MDDs deliver impressive query performance by pre-calculating or pre-consolidating transactional data rather than calculating on-the-fly. (MDDs pre-calculate and store every measure at every hierarchy summary level at load time and store them in efficiently indexed cells for immediate retrieval.) However, to fully pre-consolidate incoming data, MDDs require an enormous amount of overhead, both in processing time and in storage. An input file of 200MB can easily expand to 5GB; obviously, a file this size takes many minutes to load and consolidate. As a result, MDDs do not scale, making them a lackluster choice for the enterprise atomic-level data in the data warehouse. However, MDDs are great candidates for >50GB departmental data marts.

To manage large amounts of data, MDD servers aggregate data along hierarchies. Not only do hierarchies provide a mechanism for aggregating data, they also provide a technique for navigation. The ability to navigate data by zooming in and out of detail is key. With MDDs, application design is essentially the definition of dimensions and calculation rules, while the RDBMS requires that the database schema be a star or snowflake. With MDDs, for example, it is common to see the structure of time separated from the repetition of time. One dimension may be the structure of a year: month, quarter, half-year, and year. A separate dimension might be different years: 1996, 1997, and so on. Adding a new year to the MDD simply means adding a new member to the calendar dimension. Adding a new year to a RDBMS usually requires that each month, quarter, half-year, and year also be added.

In General

Usually, a scalable, parallel database is used for the large, atomic, organizationally-structured data warehouse, and subsets or summarized data from the warehouse are extracted and replicated to proprietary MDDs. Because MDD vendors have enabled *drill-through* features, when a user reaches the limit of what is actually stored in the MDD and seeks more detailed data, he/she can *drill through* to the detail stored in the enterprise database. However, the drill-through functionality usually requires creating views for every possible query.

As relational database vendors incorporate sophisticated analytical multidimensional features into their core database technology, the resulting capacity for higher performance scalability and parallelism will enable more sophisticated analysis. Proprietary database and nonintegrated relational OLAP query tool vendors will find it difficult to compete with this integrated ROLAP solution.

Both storage methods have strengths and weaknesses—the weaknesses, however, are being rapidly addressed by the respective vendors. Currently, data warehouses are predominantly built using RDBMSs. If you have a warehouse built on a relational database and you want to perform OLAP analysis against it, ROLAP is a natural fit. This isn't to say that MDDs can't be a part of your data warehouse solution. It's just that MDDs aren't currently well-suited for large volumes of data (10-50GB is fine, but anything over 50GB is stretching their capabilities). If you really want the functionality benefits that come with MDD, consider subsetting the data into smaller MDD-based data marts.

When deciding which technology to go for, consider:

❏ Performance
How fast will the system appear to the end-user? MDD server vendors believe this is a key point in their favor. MDD server databases typically contain indexes that provide direct access to the data, making MDD servers quicker when trying to solve a multidimensional business problem. However, MDDs have significant performance differences due to the differing ability of data models to be held in memory, sparsity handling, and use of data compression. And, the relational database vendors argue that they have developed performance improvement techniques, such as IBM's DB2 Starburst optimizer and Red Brick's Warehouse VPT STARindex capabilities. (Before you use performance as an objective measure for selecting an OLAP server, remember that OLAP systems are about effectiveness (how to make better decisions), not efficiency (how to make faster decisions).)

❏ Data volume and scalability
While MDD servers can handle up to 50GB of storage, RDBMS servers can handle hundreds of gigabytes and terabytes. And, although MDD servers can require up to 50% less disk space than relational databases to store the same amount of data (because of relational indexes and overhead), relational databases have more capacity. MDD advocates believe that you should perform multidimensional modeling on summary, not detail, information, thus mitigating the need for large databases.

In addition to performance, data volume, and scalability, you should consider which architecture better supports systems management and data distribution, which vendors have a better user interface and functionality, which architecture is easier to understand, which architecture better handles aggregation and complex calculations, and your perception of open versus proprietary architectures. Besides these issues, you must also consider which architecture will be a more strategic technology. In fact, MDD servers and RDBMS products can be used together—one for fast response, the other for access to large databases.

Multiple Vendors or Single Solution Provider?

Other than IBM, few vendors are able to offer a complete data warehousing solution that includes complete support from design through implementation, as well as the tools necessary to design, develop, and deploy the data warehouse. Several companies, including SAS, NCR, and Prism, offer close-to-complete solutions. The single vendor solution offers high levels of integration and cooperation. Information exchange between components is centrally managed and a constant look and feel can be maintained. Also, it is likely that an overall price will be negotiable. From the business angle, this has to be seen as a good strategy.

IBM provides a seamless, end-to-end, client/server, parallel DBMS total solution based on one-stop shopping, from the parallel DBMS to object-based development tools, connectivity, and system management for heterogeneous databases, as well as IBM and third-party applications (see Figure 4-1). Hardware can also be provided. No other vendor can provide the breadth and depth of 7x24 service and support, project management, and partnering with customers that IBM can provide for parallel environments. IBM has been, and still is, the world's largest software company and the world's largest database company. It provides free- and fee-based services, as well as free bundled products for parallel environments.

The *best-of-breed* idea is diametrically opposed to the single vendor solution. The aim is to build an environment that fits the requirements of the organization. There is no compromise between databases and tools to support it, and the selected products are those best able to fulfill the criteria for functionality and price. However, the main point to consider here is the overall expense of buying best-of-breed solutions. The purchase of separate products does reduce the bargaining power for license costs.

The *staying power* of a vendor is as important as the functional characteristics of a product. Numerous information technology consolidations, restructuring, and mergers have resulted in software products being shelved or no longer marketed and supported. If you are to make the investment in data warehouse software and tools, ask for assurances that the products will continue to be supported, enhanced, and improved. This commitment is demonstrated by code quality, frequency of releases, the existence of user groups, and the vendor's ability to provide technical, educational, installation, and international service support. Other possible indicators include the vendor's level of sales and number of technical employees, years in business, sales offices, and customer installations.

Best-of-breed or single vendor depends upon the company—in an environment that is not heavily technical, it is best to identify a single vendor and use the services and support offering of that vendor for a complete solution. When technical expertise is available in an organization, spend time watching the market and choosing the products that provide the best fit for the organization.

Identifying the Pieces of the Puzzle

Ready to assemble the pieces of your data warehouse? In this chapter, we'll identify the best-of-breed products, the most competitive technologies, and the companies that can provide the technology you need to deploy your data warehouse.

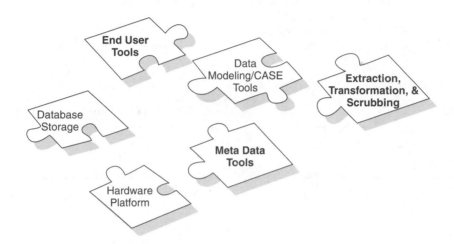

Database Storage

Database discussions and decisions initially revolve around the advantages and disadvantages of MDD (Essbase, Oracle Express, and Pilot) versus RDBMS (Oracle, Informix, DB2, Red Brick, Sybase, and Teradata)—which we discussed in the previous section of this chapter. After choosing the data warehouse archi-

tecture, you must then filter through each vendor's product line to determine which best fits your needs. Valid performance comparisons of one DBMS versus another must take into account a wide range of factors, including the operating system, the speed of the I/O devices and the CPU, as well as how much and how effectively parallel processing can be used. For example, you can compare partitioning schemas, levels of parallelism, optimizers, and explains to help with the decision-making as shown in Tables 4–2, 4–3, and 4–4.

Table 4–2 Comparing DBMS Partitioning Schemas

DBMS	Partitioning Schemas
IBM DB2 MVS	data value
IBM DB2 PE	hash, data value, and schema
Informix DSA	round robin, data value, and residue class
Sybase MPP	hash, data value, and schema
Teradata	hash
Red Brick	data value
Oracle	partitioned views, hash (data value and schema in Oracle 8)

Table 4–3 Comparing DBMS Levels of Parallelism

	DB2 MVS	DB2 PE	Informix	Oracle	Sybase MPP	Teradata
Table Scan	cond	yes	yes	cond	yes	yes
Index Scan	cond	yes	yes	cond	yes	yes
Join	cond	yes	yes	cond	cond	yes
Sort	no	yes	yes	cond	yes	yes
Insert	no	yes	yes	no	yes	yes
Update	no	yes	no	no	yes	yes
Delete	no	yes	no	no	yes	yes
Load	no	partial	manual	manual	yes	yes
Index-ing Strategies	cluster	bitmap to btree	btree/ cluster	btree/ cluster, bitmap to btree	bitmap to btree	bitmap

Table 4–4 Comparing DBMS Optimizers and Explains

DBMS	Optimizers	Explains
IBM DB2 MVS	excellent	excellent
IBM DB2 PE	excellent	excellent
Informix	fair	excellent
Oracle	good	good
Sybase	fair	good
Teradata	good	excellent
Red Brick	good	poor

IBM, Informix, and Oracle have begun using the terminology *Universal Server* in their product naming. The RDBMS is under technology pressure from users who demand that the RDBMS understand time series, moving averages, and/or rankings. As a result, a new RDBMS is emerging, called a Universal Server, that allows information technology organizations, RDBMS suppliers, and ISVs to extend the RDBMS with complex data (images, sounds, and video), functions, and access techniques. Direct business benefits of Universal Server technology include greater programmer productivity and faster execution and response times for complex data.

The Aberdeen Group believes that Universal Server technology will become widespread over the next two to three years as RDBMS suppliers bring their products to market, making Universal Server technology one of the most significant advances in RDBMS technology over the next decade. The Aberdeen Group defines a Universal Server as "an RDBMS that offers users the ability to efficiently access complex data types—including functions related to particular data types—and support open, extensible user-defined data types." The Universal Server architecture has an RDBMS framework, enabling specific application customization, such as Internet OLTP. In addition, the Universal Server architecture shouldn't require major rewrites or upgrades. New complex data type capabilities are simply added to an existing RDBMS, with minimal effects on a production system. Thus, the Information Technology group has full control over how much and how rapidly it takes advantage of the new functions.[1]

1. See "Universal Servers: RDBMS Technology for the Next Decade", *Aberdeen Group Technology Viewpoint*, June 3, 1995, v9, n13.

Key reference information about each of the major database vendors follows; this information should not substitute for researching and investigating the vendors' products, however.

Oracle: Oracle7
(Note that Oracle 8 was released on Solaris and Windows NT as this book went to print, but 7.3 retains the majority of installs.)

Oracle has numerous installs with concurrent user populations of more than 1,000 and probably the greatest installed base of parallel RDBMSs today, both in terms of shared-everything systems running on UNIX SMP hardware and shared-disk systems running on clusters and MPP. Oracle is enhancing OLTP scalability by harnessing a smaller number of powerful 64-bit processors with memory spaces of up to 8GB, well beyond the 2GB address limit of most 32-bit systems. Oracle has licensed well over 1,000 copies of Oracle Parallel Server (its shared disk architecture), with the majority of these licenses installed on clusters.

Oracle provides intra-query parallelism via the Parallel Query option (can be used on SMP platforms). It is a process-based model, with each user connecting to a query coordinator, which calls on a number of query slaves, usually resident in a pool, to produce the effects of vertical and horizontal parallelism. The Parallel Query option provides a parallel table scan and some utilities, but no parallel index scans, inserts, deletes, or updates. What the Parallel Query Option can parallelize depends on a number of factors like the system load and the optimizer parse sequence. Only Table Scan and Row Redistribution are parallelized on an inter-node basis.

Oracle uses a shared-everything model on SMP platforms and a shared-disk model on MPP platforms. It can also combine the two models in clusters or hybrid SMP/MPP environments. The shared-everything style is the obvious choice for SMP platforms and works well, but by going with shared-disk, Oracle is out of step with the industry. (Note that if implemented correctly, shared-nothing on MPP platforms should be superior to shared disk for intra-query parallelism. The ability of individual products to: 1) maximize the use of potential processing power; 2) reduce the volume of internal data flows; and 3) use intelligent join and aggregation techniques has a major impact on performance.) Oracle has enhanced v7.3 to perform more local sorting and joining and more widespread balancing of processing requirements across nodes. It has also introduced disk affinity for individual processors on MPP systems, emulating a shared-nothing model for a stage in the overall query process. The shared-disk architecture requires emulation code (Virtual Shared-Disk - VSD) for it to run on the SP, obviously impacting performance.

Features of v7.3

Oracle v7.3 supports *parallel execution* of UNION and UNION ALL operations that are commonly used in decision support applications to assemble result sets from multiple underlying tables. Other features include parallel execution of NOT IN conditions and improved parallel execution of GROUP BY operations. The cost-based optimizer incorporates parallel execution considerations when determining query execution plans. The optimizer chooses intelligent heuristic defaults for parallelism based on the number of available processors and the disk devices that store table data. Access path choices and table scan versus index access, for example, take into account the degree of parallelism available, resulting in plans that are optimized for parallel execution.

V7.3 supports *partition views*. (A partition view allows a table, typically one with a large amount of data, to be broken into multiple smaller tables (or partitions) and then presented to applications as a single object through the use of a UNION ALL view.) Doing data management operations such as data loads, index creation, and data purges at the partition level, rather than on the entire table, results in significantly reduced times for these operations. And, since the partitions are independent of each other, the availability of a partition of data does not affect access to the rest of the data in the partition view. Oracle 8 further implements partitioning.

V7.3 incorporates *bit-mapped indexing* as an integrated server capability, delivering performance benefits to decision support applications. (Bit-mapped indexes coexist with and complement other available indexing schemes, including standard B-tree indexes, clustered tables, and hash clusters. Bit-mapped indexes are ideally suited for column data having a small number of possible values and enhance performance for ad hoc queries involving logical operations on these columns.) Faster *index rebuilds* are also available via a new operation that uses an existing index, rather than the base table, as the data source for rebuilding an index. Since the indexed data is typically much smaller, use of this facility will substantially reduce the time for index rebuilds.

IBM: DB2

IBM's DB2 for MVS is a proven solution for organizations planning to implement enterprise-level OLTP systems supporting 10,000 user connections with database sizes up to 3TB. DB2 is capable of transaction rates of 200 transactions per second (tps), and some organizations, using DB2 Data Sharing on Parallel Sysplex, have implemented DB2 systems that support 500 tps. DB2 for MVS is particularly effective in transaction processing (TP) monitor support and running large batch workloads. DB2 for MVS v.4.2 enables online data reorganization, enabling support for 24x365 operations. And, v4.2 also supports intra-query parallelism. DB2 for MVS may lack the sophistication of the intra-query parallelism of Teradata and up-and-coming UNIX-based products (for example, IBM DB2 Parallel Edition, Informix, and Oracle), but in recent releases, it has been closing the functionality gap, although it still lacks such features as parallel hash joins and parallel sorts.

DB2 for AIX is targeted at the mainstream OLTP market, providing an efficient multi-threaded architecture and good scalability on SMP hardware. DB2 for AIX v.2 (which has been ported to OS/2, other UNIX platforms, and Windows NT) is a shared-everything software architecture, using a resource-efficient, multi-threaded server based on threads that can be either IBM's own portable threads package or the native operating system threads package. DB2 for AIX Parallel Edition is a shared-nothing software model that is almost exclusively targeted at shared-nothing SP hardware, although it is feasible to run it on an SMP RS/6000 by configuring it with multiple logical software nodes. (An example of a shared-nothing software architecture running on a shared-everything hardware architecture.) Both DB2 and Parallel Edition support IBM's high-availability software (HACMP).

Features of IBM's DB2 Universal Database
The latest version of DB2 is DB2 Universal Database 5.0, a multimedia, Web-enabled database, scaling from Intel to UNIX platforms, as well as uniprocessors to SMP to MPP. DB2 Universal Database combines the relational feature set of DB2 Common Server Version 2.1 with the parallel processing and clustering, query performance, and very large database support of DB2 Parallel Edition Version 1.2. Support for object-relational data types (such as image, video, audio, and text) is integrated into the database via user-defined functions and user-defined data types. Using user-defined functions (UDFs) and user-defined types (UDTs), customers can define data environments, simplifying application development.

We've only seen the DB2 beta, but it reveals an easy-to-use graphical management interface and performance enhancements, as well as accessibility in Web environments on par with Informix Universal Server. The architecture of this new version of DB2 is somewhat similar to Informix Universal Server. Like Informix's DataBlade technology, IBM's Extenders let application developers manipulate multimedia data types. DB2 Universal Database includes four Extenders that handle text, image, audio, and video data. In addition, IBM is working with third-party vendors to create Extenders for additional data types. DB2 Universal Database also joins the growing number of database products that currently let developers store business logic and rules as objects. Using the

Table Function, DB2 SQL cannot only process external data, but can also capture nonrelational data. As with competing database products from Oracle and Sybase, IBM's DB2 Universal Database now supports rollup and cube features for grouping data and performing cross-tabulations, respectively. Also, built-in functions provide rapid query performance by optimizing SQL execution.

DB2 Universal Database connects easily to a multi-tiered or Web environment. Version 5.0 can support Java and Java Database Connectivity (JDBC) and includes the Net.Data add-on to assist developers with creating Java applets and connecting to DB2 databases via JDBC. You can deploy applets created with Net.Data to major Web servers, such as Microsoft and Netscape. To access and manage data on large legacy systems, this version supports IBM's Distributed Relational Database Architecture (DRDA). This allows a DB2 Universal Database to connect to and interact with DB2 data on platforms that support DRDA, such as MVS and AS/400. DB2 Universal Database includes Lotus Approach, which provides additional decision support capabilities not available in DB2.

One of DB2 Universal Database's greatest strengths is its capability to easily scale data from laptops to clustered environments and massively parallel processors. Boosts to memory management include large buffer pools and 64-bit memory support. DB2 Universal Database also features expanded support for very large database handling and extension of databases across multiple nodes and partitions. The Control Center graphical database management toolset makes administering a DB2 database easy, integrating performance configuration, monitoring, and operation scheduling into the easy-to-use Control Center interface.

What's Next?
IBM and Arbor Software are integrating Arbor Software's Essbase OLAP Engine with DB2 (via Extenders) to create the IBM DB2 OLAP server. The IBM DB2 OLAP server allows access to multidimensional data through Web browsers, ensuring that customers can perform powerful analyses via the Web. Features include sophisticated OLAP calculations, comprehensive OLAP navigation features, complex query support, and multi-user read/write functionality.

Informix: OnLine
Informix's Dynamic Scalable Architecture (DSA) strategy led to the development of the OnLine Extended Parallel Server, OnLine Dynamic Server, and OnLine Workgroup Server. The Informix shared-nothing architecture is implemented by means of multi-threaded co-servers that reside at each node and own different database partitions. The degree of inherent parallelism is impressive, as is the

join technology. Informix has added the ability to manage database partitions at a group level *(db slices)*, which effectively trades control over data placement for easier manageability. The OnLine Extended Parallel Server is designed for high-volume OLTP environments that need to utilize loosely coupled or shared-nothing computing architectures composed of SMP clusters or MPP systems. The OnLine Dynamic Server is designed for high-volume OLTP environments that require replication, mainframe-level database administration tools, and the performance delivered by Informix's parallel data query technology (PDQ). PDQ enables parallel table scans, sorts and joins, parallel query aggregation for decision support and parallel data loads, independent builds, and backups and restores. This server supports SMP, but not MPP (the difference between the OnLine Dynamic and OnLine Extended Parallel servers). The OnLine Workgroup Server is designed for a smaller number of user connections (32 concurrent) and lower transaction volume.

Informix is pursuing a number of strategies to strengthen and differentiate its core database products, including increasing the range of data types that Informix RDBMS engines can handle, establishing Informix engines as data warehousing platforms, making Informix servers attractive for use in mobile computing, taking advantage of the Internet to reach new database markets, and exploiting other emerging technologies such as SmartCards.

Features of Informix's Universal Server

The Informix Universal Server combines the scalability of Informix's DSA with DataBlade technology. DataBlade modules are plug-in object extensions that enable Universal Server to manage complex data types such as video, audio, image, spatial, time-series, and HTML. DataBlade modules provide data storage and management functionality attuned to the needs of a specific application and can be used independently or in conjunction with one another. Customers can choose from a wide selection of Informix and third-party DataBlade modules, or they can design their own, to meet their own unique data management requirements.

Informix's connectivity products include Universal Web Connect, an open platform that provides high-performance connectivity between Web servers and database servers. Universal Web Connect enables Web developers to create intelligent Web applications that dynamically deliver Web pages to a corporation's Internet, intranet, and extranet users. Universal Web Connect features include a set of session and connection management services to ensure optimized database connectivity. Enterprise Gateway Manager allows Informix application users and developers to transparently access Oracle, Sybase, DB2, and other non-Informix databases. Enterprise Gateway for EDA/SQL allows tools and applications running on UNIX and Microsoft Windows to access data located anywhere in the enterprise. It provides both SQL and remote procedure call access to over 60 relational and non-relational data sources on 35 different hardware platforms and operating systems. And finally, CLI is a call-level interface that enables application developers to dynamically access Informix database servers, eliminating the need for an SQL preprocessor and for the recompilation of source code for each independent data source. Based on Microsoft's Open Database Connectivity (ODBC) architecture, CLI provides an industry-standard means of connecting to Informix data.

Application development products include the Data Director for Visual Basic, which enables developers to rapidly prototype, build, and extend workgroup and enterprise applications by automating the data access operations of the client. Data Director for Java (previously Jworks) is a drag-and-drop Java development component that allows developers to build database-aware Java applets (supports SQL3), enabling organizations to use Internet or intranet applications for data access. Finally, NewEra is a component-based, object-oriented architecture which includes a database application language, facilities for distributed, partitioned applications and team-oriented development, OLE and ActiveX support and Java code generation, and a suite of visual programming tools.

What's Next?
Informix acquired the San Francisco-based Stanford Technology Group (STG), known for its MetaCube product, which presents a multidimensional view of underlying relational data through the use of an intermediary meta data layer. This lets users of Informix RDBMS servers carry out online analytical processing (OLAP) by using the MetaCube technology. Informix also partnered with Netscape Communications Corporation to include the Informix OnLine Workgroup Server RDBMS as the development and deployment database for Netscape's LiveWire Pro.

Microsoft: SQL Server
With the release of Windows NT v3.51 and additional RDBMS development and tuning, SQL Server v6.0 provided inter-query OLTP scalability on SMP hardware with up to four processors, as well as parallel I/O. SQL Server uses a shared-everything software architecture and its operation is highly integrated with the NT operating system threads facilities. Microsoft is working with hardware partners such as Compaq, Digital, HP, NCR, and Tandem to produce high-availability clusters with implementations available on Compaq and Digital with

SQL Server v.6.5. This is a two-node, shared disk hardware model, but SQL Server does not have a shared disk software model and cannot give concurrent database access from the two nodes. It only has the ability to failover between servers and nodes.

In a high-availability challenge to UNIX clusters for medium-sized systems, Microsoft has introduced the first stage of its Microsoft Cluster Server, superseding hardware vendors' APIs and extending shared-disk hardware capability beyond two nodes. But, Microsoft still has the unenviable tasks of dismantling its integrated SQL Server software that relies on a single ANSI SQL-based interface and replacing it with a series of interacting components, including a separate data manager, lock manager, and transaction services manager.

Features of SQL Server 6.5
SQL Server 6.5 refines the multi-threaded parallel architecture of SQL Server 6.0 to improve performance and scalability. TPC benchmark results published by Microsoft on April 5, 1996, show SQL Server 6.5 to be 48% faster than version 6.0 running on a similarly configured Compaq ProLiant 4500 5/133 four-processor server. Some of this performance improvement is due to the addition of scaleable locking architecture, Dynamic Locking, which combines the use of page- and row-level locking for optimum performance and concurrency.

SQL Server 6.5 also introduced transparent distributed transactions (transparent two-phase commit). Programming interfaces supported include Transact-SQL, DB-Library, ODBC, XA, and OLE Transaction. SQL Server can publish information to other databases, including Oracle, IBM DB2, Sybase, Microsoft Access, and other ODBC-compatible databases. New online analytical processing (OLAP) query extensions, CUBE and ROLLUP, simplify the retrieval of multi-dimensional information. A new *data pipe* capability, enabled by the INSERT...EXEC statement, lets SQL Server 6.5 populate tables with information from other SQL Server machines and data sources.

SQL Enterprise Manager includes integrated schema and data transfer capabilities, administration tools for DTC, an extensible toolbar and menu for add-ins, support for SNMP traps and alerts, and a DBA Assistant that automates the creation of scheduled maintenance operations.

Red Brick: Warehouse
Red Brick is a good choice when implementing a departmental data mart (using a star schema). Red Brick's DBMS is also a good fit when capturing large amounts of transaction detail data where the record sizes are small (for example, point of sale). The Red Brick RDBMS is well-proven for dimensional analysis, application-specific data marts of up to 400GB, and 40 concurrent users.

Red Brick derives its query performance from a mixture of one-pass joins on star schemas, internal intra-query parallelism, and bit-mapped indexing. Users build sets of summary tables to match the detail tables and enable a form of drill-down. Sufficient memory is particularly important for performance; Red Brick, unlike most RDBMSs, does not provide a global buffer cache. Instead, users buffer relevant data in their own process spaces, potentially sharing I/O during retrieval via the SuperScan feature. During query parallelization, Red Brick holds intermediate result sets in memory, and if necessary, writes them to disk as spill files, adversely affecting performance. Queries are constrained by the database design and ad hoc queries are difficult to achieve. Red Brick is a query-only environment and backup and recovery is not available (per query).

Red Brick's DBMS is specifically designed as a data warehousing DBMS, using a non-relational data store. Because of this specific design, Red Brick cannot handle OLTP or mixed workloads. The use of the data store allows optimization for fast query processing through single-pass, multi-table joins; however, to get the speedup advantage, data must be reorganized from traditional relational schemas and converted to star schema designs and query-only usage.

Through a mixture of inter- and intra-query parallelism, Red Brick has shown an ability to harness up to 12 processor UNIX SMP systems. Tables are partitioned into segments that can be organized by range (typically a time series) or by hash function. Segmentation enables range-based data to be easily loaded into or dropped from the database. The loader performs well and can load segments in parallel while also creating aggregate tables and helping resolve referential integrity issues. The likelihood of data skew with range-based segments can be reduced on SMP platforms by striping the data using operating system-level facilities. However, the most granular level of locking is at the table level and transaction logging is nonexistent. These constraints make the DBMS unwieldy for hash-based segmentation and frequent, nonbatch-oriented data loading.

Features of Red Brick Warehouse 5.0

Red Brick's TARGETindex bit-mapped indexing includes a full family of index types to handle all kinds of data, whether of low cardinality (for example, male or female) or of high cardinality (for example, social security numbers). Red Brick's Continually Adaptive Indexing extends TARGETindex technology to provide indexes which automatically and continually adapt to the data that is being indexed. V5 automatically selects the optimal index type on a per value, not per index, basis.

V5 incorporates analysis algorithms which identify references to indexes and identify and simplify redundancies, contradictions, and tautologies, thus improving complex SQL query performance. V5 adds another advanced join technique, hybrid hash join, which includes sophisticated optimizations such as full sub-join recursion (needed to efficiently handle very large joins), role reversal (needed to efficiently join dissimilarly-sized tables), and bit filtering (needed to dramatically improve hash join efficiency). V5 also includes analysis techniques which identify, rewrite, and reschedule subqueries to increase complex query performance.

Sybase: SQL Server
Sybase had major problems with SQL Server v10. First, it was beset by software quality problems and then as those began to settle down, the processor scalability issue blew up (OLTP scalability stopped at six processors, making Sybase non-competitive). With SQL Server v11, Sybase has started to address both of these issues. SQL Server v11 is strong on throughput and resource efficiency for small and medium-sized OLTP systems and is building credibility for large concurrent user populations. The largest user populations now surpass 1,000 connected users, with database sizes of up to 500GB. And, SQL Server v11 is capable of providing good inter-query scalability for OLTP on SMP systems up to 16 processors. Sybase is following Oracle (as well as DB2 and Informix) by trying to support the OLTP, data warehousing, Internet, and other potential markets (including low-end DBMS, mobile client/server, and SQL Server on NT).

Features of Sybase SQL Server v11
The most significant scalability enhancements for SQL Server v11 include architectural improvements to the logging, locking, and data cache subsystems. SQL Server v11 uses an enhanced logging system, the Private Log Cache (PLC), to reduce the contention on the log semaphore. In the PLC—an area of memory private to a user's task—log records are built and stored before being posted to the log file. The PLC may hold multiple log records for a single transaction before they are flushed to the log file through the log semaphore. When a transaction commits or the memory fills with log records, the PLC is flushed to the log file. Because the log records for a complete transaction are immediately transferred through the log semaphore, contention on the log semaphore becomes almost nonexistent, thus increasing transaction throughput.

Memory manager is enhanced via multiple data caches, sequential prefetch (using large I/Os), a new fetch-and-discard buffer replacement strategy, full user control in configuring each cache, and automatic query optimizer support. Additionally, SQL Server v11 has a background process that better utilizes spare CPU cycles and offloads a portion of the work from OLTP applications. SQL Server v11 also lets users create multiple data caches and partition the memory available for the data caches into a site-specified number of named caches. Each named cache can be reserved for specific applications (databases or database objects) and can be configured (in terms of the block size of I/O and the overall size of the cache) for specific applications.

NCR: Teradata

NCR's Teradata RDBMS has a strong track record for satisfying large and complex DSS requirements through the use of parallel technology. With the introduction of Teradata v2, a major software-only re-implementation of the product, NCR sheds the *proprietary* hardware and operating system label that was always attached to the Teradata name. However, Teradata still has some major difficulties to overcome, including Teradata's proprietary history, the continued lock-in to NCR hardware (NCR not being one of the mainstream DBMS vendors), and the divestiture of NCR from AT&T. Teradata doesn't have much presence in the mainstream RDBMS market. And, although the Teradata-related hardware and services business is important to NCR, NCR is still promoting a mixed data warehouse RDBMS portfolio via partnerships with Informix, Oracle, and Sybase.

Features of Teradata v2

Teradata v2 is a capable and scaleable DBMS for data warehousing. In particular, it is the most proven DBMS for complex DSSs and data warehouses with VLDBs and very large concurrent user populations. With v2, NCR delivered a UNIX-based product and added enhancements to provide improved support for databases as they extend beyond 10TB. Improvements to the hashing algorithm to reduce contention and spread the workload more evenly across multiple processors enhanced its ability to tackle VLDBs. V2 architecture has the ability to effectively allocate processors to disk partitions at startup time, enabling greater ability to balance the system for performance purposes while enhancing flexibility. This flexibility enables administrators to deal with unplanned processor and disk failure, as well as planned maintenance downtime. High-availability protection against disk failure is provided by the use of RAID 5 disk units, or the fallback option that mirrors a disk. Teradata v2 protects against processing node failure by failing over database partitions that were being controlled by logical software nodes (termed VPROCs by Teradata) to VPROCs on a surviving SMP node within the same cluster.

End-user Tools

Our method for selecting end-user tools includes:

1. Gathering and weighting end-user requirements
2. Using the end-user requirements to write a Request For Information, or RFI (which should include your feature weighting)
3. Determining which vendors should receive your RFI
4. Scoring RFI responses and evaluating vendor demonstrations

Query & Reporting tools enable users to access enterprise data for reporting and graphing without having to know SQL. Query tools enable users to answer questions in lists. For example, a user could ask (and expect an answer to) something similar to: "Retrieve all products costing between $50 and $125 purchased from ABC Supply Company on May 1, 1996." *OLAP* tools, on the other hand, are multidimensional. OLAP tools empower the business user to look for causative factors exploring *Why?* and *What if?* versus the traditional *What?*. For example, one could ask: "Compared to the previous year, how have the last 12 months of increased advertising expenditures impacted my product sales in NYC compared to San Francisco?"

Information technology *development tools* provide screen painters with 4GLs to provide query, reporting, graphing, and multidimensional analysis without programming, but they result in less flexible black-box information technology applications.

OLAP tools include:

1. *ROLAP databases*: Oracle, Sybase, Informix's MetaCube family, RedBrick, Ingres, and DB2

2. *Multi-dimensional*: Arbor's Essbase, Oracle's Express, Pilot's Analysis Server

3. *High-end tools*: Information Advantage's DecisionSuite Server, MicroStrategy's DSS Server

4. *Desktop ROLAP tools*: Cognos' PowerPlay, Brio's Query[2], Business Objects' Business Objects, PLATINUM's Forest & Trees, and IQ Software's IQ/Vision

5. *Desktop MDD tools*: Cognos' PowerPlay, Brio's Brio.Insight, Business Objects' Business Objects, Microsoft's Excel, Lotus' Lotus 1-2-3, Oracle's Express, Pilot's Desktop

---

2. Brio, Business Objects, and Cognos' PowerPlay integrate query, reporting, and OLAP functionalities.

Query and reporting tools include:

6.   Cognos' Impromptu, Brio's Query, Business Objects' Business Objects, Seagate's Crystal Reports, Borland's ReportSmith, and Software AG's Esperant.

Figure 4–3 indicates where each category of tool fits into your data warehouse architecture. (Note that the numeric indications in the text correspond to the numbers in the illustration.)

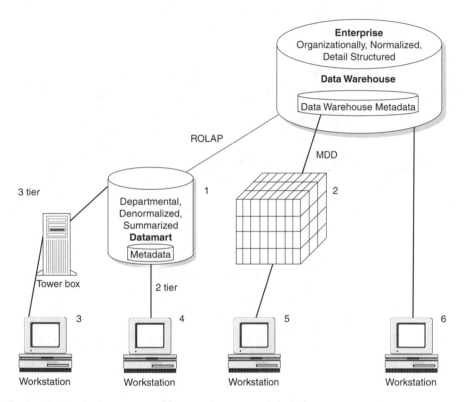

Figure 4–3   Determining which category of front end access tools best fits your needs.

Development tools include:

- Powersoft's PowerBuilder, Microsoft's Visual Basic, SAS's SAS System components, Seagate's Holos, and Oracle's Developer2000 (as well as the tools falling under the query and reporting category and the OLAP high-end, desktop-ROLAP, and desktop-MDD tools).

After determining which category of tool best meets your end-user's requirements, review feature comparison charts (similar to Tables 4-5 and 4-6) to choose the most appropriate vendor to whom to submit an RFI.

Table 4–5 Comparison Chart

OLAP Tools

Features	Integrated		Desktop		ROLAP		IQ/Vison	Mult-Dimensial DB (MDD)			Other		
	Brio	BusObj	Cognos PowerPlay	Pablo	Information Advantage	Micro Strategy		Pilot	Oracle Express	Arbor Essbase	Sas	Holos	Platinum
Query/reporting/olap integrating	◐	●	●[1]	√	√	√	○	√	√	○[3]	√	○	○
Graphing integration	◐	●	●	○	○	○	○	○	○	○	○	√	○
DW metadata integration	●	○	-	-	-	-	○	-	○	√	√	-	-
Collaboration	◐	○	○	○	●	◐	√	○	○	○	√	√	○
Ease of use	◐	●	●	√	◐	◐	◐	○	○	●	√	○	○
Security	○	○	●[2]	√	●	◐	√	√	√	√	√	○	√
Scalability	◐	◐	◐	√	●	√	√	-	√	-	√	√	√
Spreadsheet integration	√	√	√	√	√	√	√	√	√	●	√	√	-
Automatic agents	-	√	√	-	◐	◐	-	-	-	●	√	-	-
Client platforms	●	√	√	○	√	√	√	○	○	○	●	○	●
Databases	●	√	●	●	◐	●	●	○	√	√	●	√	◐
Cost	○	◐	◐	◐	√	○	○	√	√	◐	-	√	√
Ease of centralized installation/maint.	◐	●	◐	√	○	○	√	√	√	√	√	√	√
Scheduling of query	√	√	√	√	◐	√	√	√	√	○[3]	√	√	√
Cancel of query	-	-	-	-	-	◐	-	√	-	-	○	√	√
Application Development	-	○	-	-	-	-	-	○	○	-	○	○	○
Briefing Books	-	○	√	-	-	-	-	√	√	◐	-	-	√
Built in Date Dim.	-	√	√	-	-	-	-	√	√	√	-	√	√
Hints on Drill	√	√	○	√	●	-	-	√	-	◐	-	√	-
Connect Multiple Databases simultan.	-	-	√	√	-	-	-	√	√	-	√	-	√
Ranking & Exceptions	○	○	●	-	●	◐	○	○	◐	●	◐	○	○
Web OLAP	4Q96	○	4Q96	-	◐	●	-	4Q96	√	●	√	-	4Q96

● Excellent   ◐ Very Good   ○ Good   √ Satisfactory   - Unacceptable

[1] With Impromptu
[3] With Crystal Reports included in next release
[2] With Informix MetaCube

Table 4–6 Query and Reporting Tools Feature Comparison Chart

	IMPROMPTU 3.0	CRYSTAL REPORTS 4.0	REPORTSMITH 2.5	ESPERANT 3.0
configure & setup	●	○	○	◕
simple select reports	◕	◕	◕	◕
complex multitable reports	◕	◕	◕	◕
power-user facilities	●	◕	◕	○
performance	◕	◕	○	-
security	◕	-	-	○
documentation	◕	○	√	√
support	◕	○	○	√
cost	○	○	◕	○

● Excellent   ◕ Very Good   ○ Good   √ Satisfactory   - Unacceptable

Hardware Platform

Choosing a hardware architecture is not as important as is the actual implementation. That is, did the vendor do a good job of building the RDBMS features that your application requires? The only way to discover this is to test your own application by building prototypes and creating and running benchmarks as proofs-of-concept for various facets of your data warehouse application. (Check into the vendor's "Quick Start" programs, which are theoretically designed to help you do this.) Even if you decide to start with a relatively large data warehouse (in the 100-200GB range), figure on the amount of data in your warehouse doubling in a year. Similarly, count on the number of users growing by an order of magnitude within two years, during which time the overall CPU cycles required to process all of the queries will grow at least 100 times. You'll need a system that can handle this growth, thus increasing your critically important return on investment (ROI).

To optimize your DBMS performance, you'll choose between two types of *parallel hardware*: symmetric parallel processing (SMP) and massively parallel processing (MPP). The difference between SMP and MPP is what is shared. In SMP, the processors share a common memory, while in MPP, the processors don't share anything. SMP machines are easier to control, while MPP machines scale much further. SMPs have multiple processors (usually up to a few dozen) that all share the same physical memory and the same memory bus (see Figure 4–4).

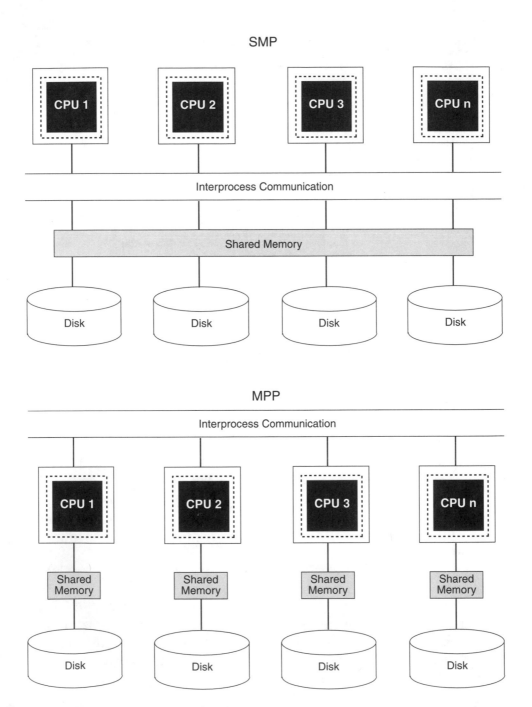

Figure 4–4 SMP versus MPP system architecture.

Because SMPs hit scalability limits when the memory bus becomes a bottleneck, hardware vendors introduced the idea of *clustering*. Clustering lets users connect multiple SMP machines (referred to as "nodes") with a very fast interconnect, enabling the machines to work as if they were a single, larger machine (see Figure 4–5). However, after clustering a few machines together (IBM's RS/6000 SP can support up to 512 nodes via one interconnect or high-speed switch), the single interconnect becomes a bottleneck. MPPs solve this problem by using a *scaleable interconnect*, where the bandwidth of the interconnect grows each time a node is added.

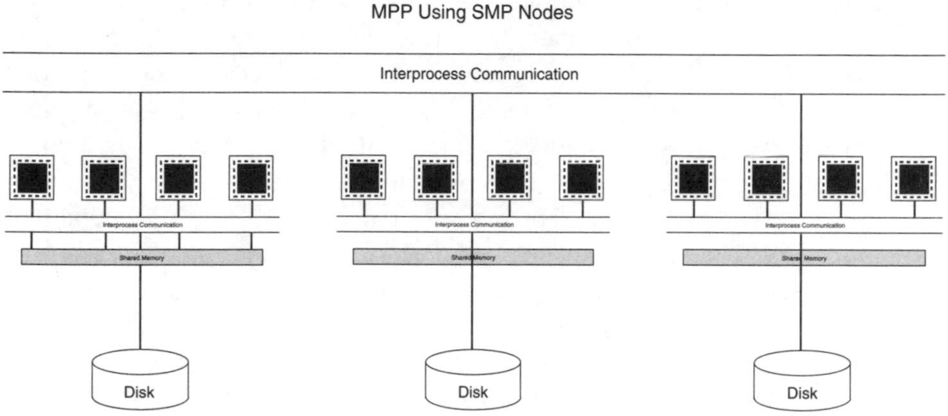

MPP Using SMP Nodes

Figure 4–5 Cluster architecture.

SMP systems combined with RDBMSs capable of intra-query parallelism are very effective for data marts, decision support applications, and data warehousing. SMP systems tend to have a lower initial cost threshold than MPP systems. And, SMP systems can support data warehouse databases of up to 200GB. The number of users that can be supported is totally dependent on what those users are attempting to do. SMP data warehouse systems have recently extended their range with the advent of 64-bit addressing and significantly faster processors, making it possible to buffer large sections of the database in memory.

MPP systems originally consisted of single-processor nodes connected via scaleable interconnects, such as the high-speed switch in the IBM SP. Although this gave a scaleable hardware configuration, it became clear by 1994 that, particularly in OLTP applications, portable RDBMS products were having limited success in harnessing the power of these systems due to the overhead of both shared-disk and shared-nothing software architectures. The problems of trying to manage numerous different instances of an RDBMS server within a single system were also becoming apparent. A solution combined the best of both worlds—SMP nodes as multiple sources of "clean," manageable power were coupled together in an MPP configuration around a scaleable, high-capacity interconnect such as a BYnet in an NCR 5100M or a mesh in an SNI/Pyramid RM1000.

The combination of MPP and data warehousing has two great advantages over the combination of MPP and OLTP. First, the creation of a new data warehousing environment is seen as dramatically less risky than entrusting new or existing mission-critical OLTP workloads to an unproven platform that is difficult to tune and manage. Second, for high-end data warehousing, with complex queries and large amounts of data, large reserves of processing power are required, and MPP technology is the only way of scaling up a single system to provide this necessary horsepower. Therefore, RDBMSs on MPP platforms such as the IBM SP provide a suitable combination for large-scale data warehouse environments. As hardware technology evolves, it is expected that uniprocessor MPP systems will go out of fashion in favor of hybrid MPP systems with a smaller number of SMP nodes. As RDBMSs are fully able to harness these platforms, users will be able to get the best of both worlds—gaining the ability to start on SMP and to continue growing the system in an evolutionary fashion, without facing any major discontinuities forced by major upgrades or platform switches.

This evolutionary move has great attraction from the RDBMS vendor's viewpoint. By combining the two architectures, it is possible to achieve a blend that builds on the advantages of both while being able to reduce any disadvantages. The easily harnessed power of an SMP can be brought to bear on any problem initially, but then, instead of reaching a plateau, it is possible to continue to provide additional processing power via MPP techniques. On the other side of the coin, the negatives of MPP technology, such as the coordination overhead and management problems—particularly if there are a large number of nodes—can usually be brought under control.

Scalable database software is the second critical component of a scaleable data warehouse. The database must be able to take advantage of multiple processors and multiple nodes within a scaleable system. All of the major vendors (including Oracle, Informix, IBM, Sybase, Teradata, and Tandem) have been developing and selling versions of their databases that leverage the underlying scaleable hardware. Parallel RDBMSs on SMP hardware provide the cleanest and most mature sources of processing power to drive medium- and large-scale OLTP applications on UNIX and MVS. The OLTP scalability of RDBMSs on SMP systems will continue to grow, based on a combination of faster processors, greater internal interconnect throughput, and 64-bit memory addressing, rather than on attempts to harness more than 24 processors. Parallel RDBMSs on SMP systems will continue to provide the most straightforward sources of power for most data marts and small to medium-sized data warehouses through 2000. The range of parallel RDBMSs based on shared memory parallel processing (SMPP) hardware architectures will continue to extend upward with the advent of 64-bit address spaces, continually improving processor speed and internal interconnect throughput on SMP systems, thereby raising the threshold for consideration of MPP. Note that your hardware choice does not dictate the RDBMS software architecture. For example, a shared-nothing hardware architecture does not mandate a shared-nothing software architecture. This may have been true in initial implementations in the 1980s, but it is no longer the case today.

Storage Subsystems

Points to consider when selecting disk, tape, and/or optical storage subsystems include cost, access type, data transfer rate, and reliability and availability. As far as *cost*, the faster the access, the more expensive the solution. Semiconductor main storage or cache memory is very expensive, disk drives or arrays (also 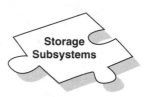 referred to as RAID, or Redundant Array of Independent Disks) are the next most expensive, followed by optical and tape drives or libraries. Cost/byte is generally inversely proportional to the capacity of the storage element. Larger disk, tape, or optical drives and fully-populated storage subsystems have the lowest cost per megabyte. In assessing cost, consider all of the cost components—adapters, enclosures, cables, software, installation, and service. It is an oversimplification to just look at the cost/byte of the drives or subsystem without assessing the total costs and balancing performance and availability needs. RAID is the most popular storage vehicle for data warehouses due to the enormity of the data. RAID 5 is the most preferred implementation or configuration where data is striped (or written in parallel) over multiple disks using a parity algorithm to re-create the data on a single disk if the main disk fails.

Data transfers can be sequential or random. Sequential access means transferring large contiguous files or records. Typically, transaction logs are written as sequential files. Tape drives are best suited for sequential access and for data file backup and recovery. Random access implies reading or writing small amounts of data at many points on a storage device. Applications requiring random access include customer service inquiries and transaction processing programs. Disk and optical drives are better suited to random transfers since they require less time to find randomly-sized and organized records.

The *data transfer rate* is the speed at which the data is written to or read from a storage device once it has been located on the device. This speed is generally expressed in MB/sec (Megabytes per second) or in I/Os (Inputs/Outputs) per second. These terms are often both used, but their meanings are different. MB/sec is a measurement of the number of bytes per second being transferred. I/Os per second refers to the number of data blocks being transferred per second.

Data transfer rates depend on the storage device and on the size of the records being moved. When data is streamed to a storage device as a very large file or collection of files (sequential access), maximum data rates are possible. There are fewer separate accesses to different addresses on the device. When large numbers of small random blocks of data are moved (random access), aggregate data rates are less. More time is spent finding and accessing the data as a part of transferring the data.

Access frequency refers to the number of times data on a storage device will be accessed in a given period. High access frequency implies a need for more reliability, minimal time to get to a data location on a storage device, as well as high data rates. Disk or optical devices are best suited to applications with high access frequency requirements.

Reliability and *availability* are extremely important considerations, particularly for mission-critical information. Reliability is the ability of the storage device to function for a stated period of time. Availability is the ratio of the total time a storage device is capable of being used to the total time it is required for use. Availability implies that data will be available from a storage device when it is required. In some applications, it may be acceptable to have an occasional failure that results in loss of data. Some applications can tolerate failures and limited down-time, but cannot tolerate data loss. Other applications are mission-critical and can afford absolutely no data loss or interruption of service. Each of the storage products offers options such as redundant adapters or controllers to provide the proper level of data availability.

Questions to Ask
When should you choose disk?
Disk is required when high performance and rapid response times are critical.

> EMC has set the standard for high-performance, high-capacity, high-availability data storage by: utilizing RAID; caching 4-8GB; using 1-32 parallel processors; and, enabling portability by allowing AS/400, UNIX, NT, and MVS to all connect to the same storage box, cutting down on network traffic.

When should you choose tape?
Tape should be used when low-cost archive of information, high-speed sequential access to data, and backup and interchange of data are required.

> *StorageTek's automated cartridge systems utilize robotic technology, enabling a storage capacity of 588 cartridges (or 600GB to 20+TB of storage) for all operating systems.*

When should you choose optical?
Optical is the solution when long-term archive of information is the primary requirement.

What about multiple device types?
Use disk/optical when:
- Requirements are for random access with medium to high performance
- Nontraditional applications such as image processing indicate a need for medium access frequency to large amounts of sequential data
- Long-term storage of information is sometimes necessary
- Data usage allows migration of less frequently accessed information to slower-speed devices
- High availability or fault tolerance is required

Use disk/tape when:
- Access to large amounts of sequential data is needed, with medium to low performance acceptable
- Large amounts of space are called for
- The time it takes to access the first byte of data is not significant; however, the performance requirements after that first access are high
- Migration of less frequently accessed information from reasonably fast media to slower-speed media is acceptable

Use tape/optical when:

- The bulk of data access is low-speed sequential
- Random access to information is required
- The time it takes to access the first byte of information is not important
- Migration of less frequently accessed information from reasonably fast media to slower-speed media is acceptable
- Data life is important

In the data warehouse environment, use RAID 5 to back up your most-accessed data (normally data spanning the last 1-3 years), use tape for standard archiving, and use tape or optical for less-frequently accessed historical data (normally data 6-10 years old). Table 4–7 compares and contrasts media characteristics.

Table 4–7 Media Characteristics

	DISK	OPTICAL	TAPE
High-speed Random Access	X		
Low-cost Random Access		X	
Sequential Access Only			X
Low-cost High-capacity		X	X
Removable Media		X	X
Permanent Recording		X	

Extraction, Transformation, and Scrubbing Tools

Data extraction actually includes triggering, filtering, extracting, transforming, integrating, cleaning, and loading data from legacy systems into the data warehouse. Data extraction ranges from simple extracts and loads to complex captures of changed data and updates to the data warehouse. Management of the flow of data into (and out of) the data warehouse (commonly referred to as extraction, transformation, and scrubbing) ensures the best return on the data.

Extraction, Transformation, & Scrubbing

Top players and products in the extraction, transformation, and scrubbing space include Evolutionary Technologies International's (ETI) ETI-EXTRACT tool suite, Prism's Warehouse Manager, and Carleton's PASSPORT. Each system effectively facilitates the initial and ongoing need to update the *enterprise data warehouse*. We also include information on Informatica's PowerMart (similar to IBM's Visual Warehouse), which is specifically designed to populate *data marts*.

Data extraction, transformation, and scrubbing from a legacy system into a data warehouse takes place every time you update your data warehouse, potentially every day. Products in this space automate the extraction, transformation, and scrubbing process—the tool reads the legacy data, identifies changes, creates load record images, migrates the data from the mainframe to the data warehouse server, sorts and re-sorts the load record images to create aggregate records, processes load exceptions, indexes the newly loaded records, and finally, publishes the data. Still wondering why you need a tool to help you out with this?

We review the Carleton PASSPORT, ETI's ETI-EXTRACT, and Prism Solutions' Warehouse Manager tools because of their dominance in the market. Using similar architectures, each automate the data extraction process, from reading legacy data to final publishing. A workstation client controls the extraction process, generating COBOL programs and associated JCL (or an IBM host reads and manipulates source data) and preparing the data for migration and loading into a target DBMS. All three products rely extensively on meta data to describe the source and target databases and to control the extraction process.

PASSPORT and Solution Warehouse Manager run on Windows, UNIX, and OS/2, while ETI-EXTRACT runs only on UNIX workstations. All three tools can read from and write to a long list of IBM mainframe systems, UNIX-flavor DBMSs, and diverse data file formats. Each tool also navigates mainframe sources with the help of data repositories and mainframe data dictionaries such as the PLATINUM Repository from PLATINUM Technology Inc. and the NATURAL LightStorm from Software AG. PASSPORT and Solution Warehouse Manager store their meta data in whatever DBMS the user wishes. ETI-EXTRACT stores its data in an internal format on a UNIX workstation only. All three vendors support the generation and execution of scripts that load data into the designated data warehouse on the target machine.

Prism's Change Manager determines what changed in the legacy data and generates new keys to automatically handle time-stamped mainframe database records and transaction logs. However, if your legacy system provides no direct clues as to what has changed (say, in a master product list), all three extraction tools accommodate a manual programming job that compares today's legacy data with yesterday's and then decides what to do with newly inserted, deleted, or changed records. Once you have written these modules, all of the extract tools will incorporate them into extraction job logic.

Data Warehouse Solution: ETI-EXTRACT, Warehouse Manager, and PASSPORT

ETI's ETI-EXTRACT targets data conversion and bridging in heterogeneous environments. Extract runs on UNIX workstations and provides developers with a GUI to generate extraction programs. The output can be in almost any language, including COBOL, C, and Assembler, and data can be imported from almost any database. Libraries already exist for DB2, Oracle, IMS, and COBOL flat files, thus accelerating the development process. Extract's monitoring function is script-driven, enabling administrators to schedule and monitor data feeds and extractions, including complex processes that are enterprisewide, covering differing time zones and/or including disparate data sources. Extract's code-generation technology and customized implementation methodology let users populate and maintain data warehouses, move to new architectures, integrate heterogeneous systems, and migrate data to new databases, platforms, and applications. A meta data facility lets users access, export, and merge meta data. Key features include versioning capabilities, a Motif-style GUI that lets users indicate how to move data through simple point-and-click interaction, a work-set facility that enables concurrent multi-user access, definable security, and data integrity protection, and a flexible reporting utility with query options for key functions such as change impact analysis.

Prism Warehouse Manager improves the speed and efficiency of building a data warehouse through automated code generation, self-documentation, and reusability. Warehouse Manager extracts operational and external data from source databases, integrates the data from the various sources, and then transforms and loads the integrated data into the target databases. An extensive selection of built-in transformations lets users perform the data conversions, summarizations, key changes, and structural changes needed to create an historical perspective of information.

Carleton PASSPORT is known for its GUI and the way it handles meta data. Carleton PASSPORT supports many operational databases as sources and exports data in flat files that can then be uploaded into any relational database. The format of the programs generated by Passport are COBOL (like Prism Warehouse Manager). Passport maps out the transformations between target and source files in a flowchart, allowing the impact of any changes to the operational database to be assessed visually. The DBA can then redefine the affected parts of the map and regenerate the COBOL transformation program. PASS-

PORT's meta data includes a description of business rules, table and column names, and statistical and version information. Users can store the meta data in the warehouse and access it via standard SQL. One of PASSPORT's strengths is its wealth of algorithms, which are designed for the processing and transformation of legacy-based data.

Another extraction tool is *IBM's Data Propagator,* which provides bi-directional change propagation between IMS and DB2 databases. Its design supports a refresh copy approach (replacing the entire copy from the source) for bulk loading or infrequent copy requests, as well as an update copy approach (applying changes since the last update) for large tables or frequent copying.

PLATINUM InfoTransport provides a high-speed tool for moving data from MVS sources (DB2, IMS, VSAM, and sequential files) to PC and UNIX servers (DB2, Sybase, Microsoft SQL Server, Informix, and Oracle), helping organizations implement distributed data processing in heterogeneous environments.

Data Mart Solution: Informatica's PowerMart

Informatica's suite of products allows for faster implementation, reduced maintenance cycles, and more intelligent decision support database design. The PowerMart suite is made up of:

- PowerMart Designer: Permits definitions of mappings and transformations using a visual interface
- Repository: Stores definitions of data marts, mappings, and transformations
- PowerMart Server: Facilitates the transformation process from the operational systems, then loads the data into the data marts
- Server Manager: Assists in configuring and managing the whole process
- Repository Manager: Manages setup and administration of the repository, and provides meta data browsing and reporting capabilities
- Power Capture: Allows a data mart to be incrementally refreshed with changes occurring in the operating system, either as they occur or on a scheduled basis by using the log mechanisms in the operational database.

Meta Data Tools

One of the most important steps in building a data warehouse is to define and create the meta data. There are three levels of meta data: data source, warehouse, and user (you can also define a business view). The meta data provides a catalogue of what's in the warehouse, as well  as the data sources that provide input to the warehouse. Meta data is key to understanding the contents and structure of a warehouse, as well as the history of changes created over time. Meta data allows users to rapidly build and productively access warehoused data. Ideally, the meta data navigator would be built on an open repository standard, enabling a range of tools to benefit from the central catalogue.

Users need to know what data is available to them and what the data means in non-technical terms. Documenting what data is available requires a catalogue of information to be maintained automatically by the products which populate the warehouse. The catalogue will support querying within itself, as well as the warehouse. For example, if a user requires information on a query which already exists relating to monthly sales figures, the user will be able to search for that query using certain keywords. The ability to invoke a host of decision support tools from this point is also a prerequisite. The catalogue should have a search capability that supports quick and easy queries by keywords, types, or values. Once the results of the query are found, the user should be able to expand the description to provide more information (meta data) on the origin and history of the data. There are several good products in this space, including Prism's Warehouse Directory, Hewlett-Packard's Intelligent Warehouse, and IBM's DataGuide.

Prism's Warehouse Directory enables you to gather, integrate, store, and manage the meta data related to your warehouse. Warehouse Directory creates a comprehensive view of the data in the warehouse (expressed in both business and technical terms) that includes information about:

- Data location
- Original data sources
- How summarizations were created
- What transformations were used
- Person responsible for data accuracy
- Queries and reports able to access the data
- How business definitions changed
- Underlying business assumptions

Warehouse Directory also supports the building of customized navigational paths for different groups of users. This enables independent querying and filtering of meta data, as well as the sharing of business names and descriptions with warehouse analysis tools. The product provides refresh/update schedules for timeliness of data. Additionally it exports physical and logical definitions and their relationships to corporate repositories.

By managing, defining, and capturing the relationships between business terms and their physical implementations, information directories enable movement between business and technical views of warehouse contents. Prism's Directory Builder gathers and integrates meta data from Prism Warehouse Directory, as well as external sources, to create the Information Directory. Once the Information Directory is created, the Directory Builder supports generation of customized directory views, as well as sharing of meta data with CASE and repository platforms. Additionally, Prism's Directory Navigator allows users to navigate the meta data in the Information Directory from a client workstation. Directory Navigator supports drill-down viewing of the meta data and displays textual summaries of highlighted entities to provide descriptive information.

HP's Intelligent Warehouse consists of software middleware and applicable administrative and end-user tools. Intelligent Warehouse (IW) is a component of OpenWarehouse—HP's overall data warehousing solution. IW features include selecting optimal existing summary tables and then using graphical displays to identify which summary tables should be populated and depopulated based on usage patterns of the warehouse. Because IW separates the physical database schema and virtual view of the warehouse, the population of new summary tables and depopulation of old summary tables have no effect on reports, saved queries, or custom decision support applications. Also, IW correctly interprets queries across multiple subject areas (known as the outer join problem).

IW manages security at the business level rather than at the physical schema level by allowing value-based security that enables users to see only those rows in which a column meets some qualification. IW supports partitioning within one or across multiple servers, enabling local data control, improved WAN performance, and manageability of extremely large data warehouses.

IBM's DataGuide provides a powerful, business-oriented solution to help end-users locate, understand, and access enterprise data. In client/server information catalogues, business meta data can be described in business terms, organized into subject areas, and customized to your workgroup's or enterprise's needs. Each DataGuide environment requires one DataGuide Administrator to set up and maintain the information catalog, then you can add as many DataGuide users as you need. The DataGuide Administrator enables you to:

- Establish your information system: Create the information catalog, set up sample information for your users, and identify an administrator and user update authority

- Classify, organize, and annotate meta data objects: Describe your organization's data from a variety of sources, such as warehouses, databases, tables, columns, queries, reports, spreadsheets, charts, and Internet documents
- Populate your information catalog: Translate information into terms with which users are familiar
- Make the information catalog convenient for users: Group objects together to make them easier to browse, add contact names so that users can find someone to ask about the information, and associate application programs with meta data objects for launching
- Expand and automate the information catalog: Use the DataGuide tag language to make it easier to work with large amounts of descriptive data at once (you can extract descriptive data from a variety of meta data sources by using provided extractors or by writing your own customized extractors)
- Integrate and manage your business meta data: Use the externally published tag language and Application Programming Interface (API)

Data Modeling / CASE Tools

DBAs have abandoned maintaining database object creation scripts in favor of maintaining a physical database design that can be constructed and versioned easily in a modeling tool. These physical modeling tools provide relief from writing endless lines of data definition language (DDL) to build database or user schemas. Instead,  a GUI is used to enter the physical design characteristics and then generate a database creation script that can be launched directly from the tool or run through the database vendor's query tool. And, referential integrity is built into most modeling tools, allowing either the declarative form of referential integrity to be used for databases that support it, or triggers to be automatically constructed to handle integrity constraints. In addition, the major modeling tools also offer reverse-engineering capabilities to let DBAs capture existing databases in a physical design.

Ideally, we would like a data modeling tool to allow us to draw all three models: (1) the high-level and mid-level logical business models, (2) the data warehouse dimensional model, and (3) the physical model.

The heavyweights duking it out in this arena are Oracle's Designer/2000, LogicWorks' ERwin, and Powersoft's Designer 6.0. With v6.0, Powersoft has added enhanced features for data warehouse and data mart design, creation, and implementation. Warehouse Architect 6.0 allows dimensional modeling, star schemas, snowflake schemas, partitioning, and aggregation. Support for fact partitioning and optimized indexing schemas is also provided. Warehouse Architect 6.0 enables extraction command scripts to automate data transfer from OLTP to the data warehouse, as well as flexible creation of structured reports through report templates.

Logic Works' ERwin/ERX Family provides a database design tool for client/ server development that lets users point and click to design a graphical entity relationship (ER) model of the business rules governing their application data. Changes to the data model can be forward-engineered to update the current database, or used to create a new database in more than 20 supported DBMSs. Tables, indexes, referential integrity (primary key and foreign key), defaults, domain/column constraints, and thousands of lines of stored procedure and trigger code are generated automatically, providing a solid foundation for new development. Using Logic Works ER*win*, you can reverse-engineer your legacy systems into models that describe all of the potential sources of your data warehouse data. A star schema dimensional model can be designed in ER*win* for implementation in your data warehouse database engine of choice.

ERwin/OPEN incorporates the core functions of the ER*win*/ERX database design tool, but contains specially tailored links to client/server application development tools, including PowerBuilder, Visual Basic, and SQLWindows. Using these links, client-side extended attributes unique to an application development environment can be defined and generated directly from an ER*win* data model. This speeds development by synchronizing server-side definitions with client-side screens. Because ER*win*/OPEN can generate client-side definitions for all three environments from the same data model, it lets developers using different tools share the same database design.

Oracle's Designer/2000 is a Windows application design solution that incorporates support for business process rendering (BPR), system analysis, software design, and code generation. Through its active repository and integration with Developer/2000, Designer/2000 allows organizations to design and rapidly deliver scaleable client/server systems that can adapt to changing business needs. Developers can develop and deploy applications with Developer/2000, or they can integrate the development process with Designer/2000 to model more complex business solutions. With Designer/2000, an executive can click on a box and listen to audio of a service phone call or watch full-motion video of a customer representative meeting with a client.

Another data modeling/CASE tool is *Evergreen CASE Tools' EasyCASE Professional*, a data- and process-modeling tool that automates the analysis and design phases of application development. EasyCASE captures system design details, letting users create graphical models of system applications. EasyCASE offers online access to an integrated data dictionary repository, rules, and extensive reporting. For forward- (schema generation) and reverse-engineering of SQL, Xbase, Access, and Paradox database applications, users can add on Easy-CASE Database Engineer.

Using object-oriented analysis and design, *Rational Software Corporation's Rational Rose* is a graphical software engineering tool that enables users to analyze, design, and implement systems that are easy to visualize and communicate. The tool set supports implementation environments ranging from C++, Smalltalk, and Ada to 4GL client/server development tools such as Power-Builder, Visual Basic, and SQL Windows. The Rational Rose family supports both the Booch '93 and Object Modeling Technique object-oriented development methods.

Silverrun's SILVERRUN-Professional Suite is a multi-platform data analysis and design tool comprised of four modules, which can be integrated or used separately. The four modules include Entity Relationship eXpert (ERX), Relational Data Modeler (RDM), Business Process Modeler (BPM), and Workgroup Repository Manager (WRM). ERX offers an embedded expert system that helps modelers create normalized data models from data structures, existing file definitions, and business rules, and can be used as a re-engineering tool. RDM includes automated functions that help ensure the production of high-quality database designs and generates schemas for 16 RDBMSs and application development tools. BPM is a process design tool for ensuring high-quality diagramming and documentation and accurate production of process flows. WRM coordinates the Silverrun toolset and supports the consolidation and sharing of dictionary information.

Popkin Software & Systems' System Architect is an application development tool that supports multiple diagramming/modeling methods. System Architect utilizes a common repository/data dictionary for the storage of model/design data and associated attributes. The support of sharing/reuse of model data through the repository leverages multiple design techniques and tracks an unlimited number of definitions, including requirements specifications, test plans, change requests, and business global/objectives. System Architect supports rules checking and balancing, CRUD matrices, leveling, audit ability, import/export, and merging of repositories and data dictionaries from multiple stand-alone users.

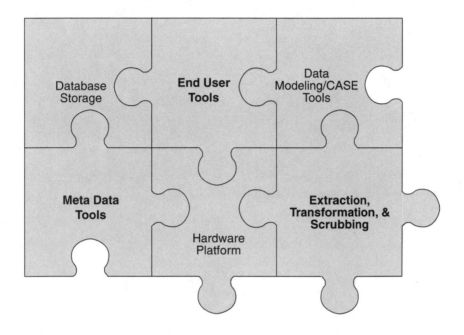

SECTION 3

BUILDING THE
DATA WAREHOUSE

Chapter 5

Understand the Data: Data Modeling

Because data warehouse teams are usually under pressure to get the warehouse up and running, one of the first steps they're tempted to skip is building the data model. Do not fall for this! One of the most critical data warehouse construction issues is *understanding the data*. And, creating a data model is the best way to understand the data. If you're determined to skip building the data model, keep the list of numbers we included in the Preface on hand, because you're going to need help.

The skill set required by a data modeler is extensive, including both technical and interpersonal skills.

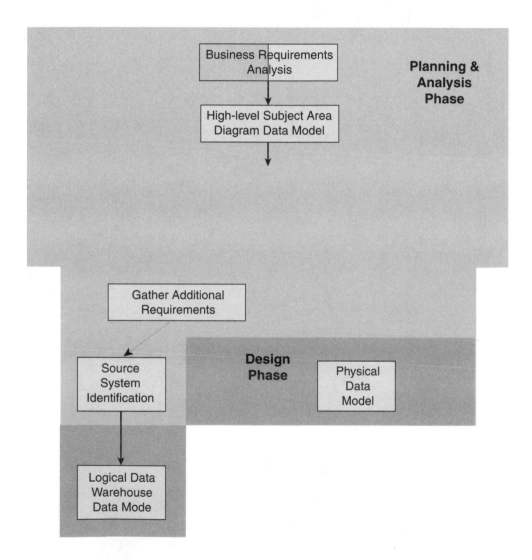

In this chapter, we walk you through the detailed steps of building the data model and identify sample deliverables for each step, including a subject area diagram, context diagram, and a logical data model. Along with building the data model, the data modeler assists in:

- Determining the high-level business requirements and creating the scope document (see Chapter 3)
- Gathering additional requirements (see Chapter 3)
- Building the physical data model (see Chapter 6)

Building the Data Model

The data model serves as your roadmap, guiding the development of the data warehouse. Building the data model ensures:

- That your scope is complete
- That the pieces of the complex data warehouse project interlock
- That the data warehouse has a solid foundation for future additions
- That redundancy is recognized and controlled

> A **data model** represents the definition, characterization, and relationships of data in a given environment. It serves as a blueprint for a solid data warehouse foundation.

Data modeling requires: 1) using data analysis techniques to discover relevant data elements, and 2) using data modeling techniques to discover the appropriate data relationships that support the current business analysis. Data modeling entails building a series of data models that provide a structured method for identifying and understanding: 1) the elements of the organization's data which must be available via decision support and 2) the optimal database architecture for timely and accurate access to this data. While building the data model, the data modeler must make decisions concerning multiple or no source systems and then identify the transformations, encoding/decoding, and conversions required during the extraction; ascertain requirements for time-variant data, ascertain data structures for the data warehouse, and determine requirements for business measures as they apply to the extraction of source system data.

The data modeler will need:

- An understanding of normalization, data dictionaries, copy books, and copy libs, as well as a background in CASE tools
- A foundation in logical data modeling, including an understanding of extraction/transformation, as well as physical constraints
- The ability to understand and then translate end-user requirements into the dimensional modeling format
- Expertise in capturing and maintaining meta data in the various tools
- Project management skills to coordinate the integration of all the meta data into a central repository, and then to follow up on the meta data issues
- Business objectivity

See Chapter 4 for a discussion of data modeling tools. We recommend purchasing a tool to decrease the potential of human error resulting from manual coding, to shorten the time required to complete the task, and to generate task documentation automatically.

Don't be misled by the generic use of the term *data model*—there is no such thing as one data model. In fact, there are four levels of data models required to build a data warehouse (see Figure 5-1), including:

- A high-level logical model, consisting of a corporate subject area diagram
- A mid-level logical model of the business subject area applicable to a particular phase of the data warehouse's construction
- The data warehouse/dimensional model, which reflects the information and analytical characteristics of the data warehouse
- The physical data model, which reflects the changes necessary to reach the performance objectives

The corporate subject area diagram consists of individual subject area diagrams that reflect various views of the corporation. These individual subject area diagrams are collected via discussions with the organizations making up your company. The total number of entities in a corporate subject area diagram is usually between 12 and 15.

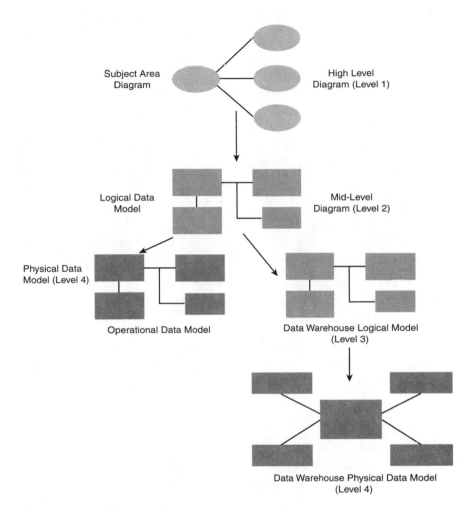

Figure 5–1 Relationship between the high-level, mid-level, data warehouse, and physical models.

Many data modeling tools allow you to create an appropriate logical data model, but do not support its transformation to a physical star schema. If you need to manually transform a logical data model into a data warehouse data model, consider:

- Removing purely operational data that isn't needed for strategic decisions (Ask yourself: "Will this particular data be used for DSS analysis?")
- Adding the element of time to the key structure, if it is not present already
- Adding derived data to enhance performance and standardization

- Accommodating levels of granularity (for example, *weekly* granularity is probably more important than operational system summarization schemes)
- Merging *like* data from different tables
- Separating data attributes based on update frequency

Level 1

Data naturally congregates around major categories relevant to the business, called subject areas or high-level entities. Data within the subject area diagram is categorized into broad, but fundamentally different, non-overlapping areas, resulting in the identification of relationships among the data and the recognition of data common to the environment. Building the subject area diagram enables you to:

- Perceive the enterprise at the highest level of abstraction
- View the impact of future development on the organization
- View the components of the enterprise independent of political or parochial perspectives

Start with the first level (see Figure 5–2), the corporate high-level subject area data model. For the corporate data model to be transformed into the data warehouse data model, the corporate data model must identify and show structure for:

- The subjects of the enterprise
- The relationships between the subjects
- A high-level entity relationship diagram (ERD)

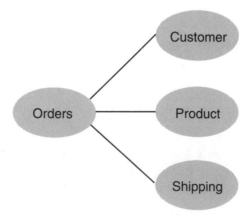

Figure 5–2 A simple high-level model.

To create the high-level diagram, you must:

- Understand the types of end-users expected to use the data warehouse (power users, executives, analysts, casual users, developers)
- Conduct high-level modeling sessions with subject matter experts and key end-users
- Review any existing data warehouse requirements documents
- Examine business forms and reports related to the subject area
- Identify which of the existing and planned data sources fall within the scope of this effort
- Identify high-level business entities and the relationships between these entities
- Create the ERD

After creating the high-level diagram, identify both the subject matter that is most critical to the end-user and the subject matter that is the most accessible for data extraction. Part of identifying these subject matters is interviewing marketing users, finance users, sales force users, operational users, first- and second-level management, and senior management. You can then list and prioritize the primary business issues facing the enterprise. To ascertain the importance of organizational data, ask the users which management needs are most important, whether there are consistent data design guidelines, what data is manageable yet significant, what data enables them to undertake and complete tasks, and/or what data is mandatory for doing their jobs.

Indirect relationships are inferred from the high-level data model; only direct relationships are shown. As such, the high-level data model does not contain any amount of detail at all; detail would only add clutter.

After recognizing the significance of the data warehousing effort, organizations sometimes bypass the first two data model levels and create the data warehouse dimensional model first and its physical data model equivalent second. This approach has proven to be successful in the short term, allowing data marts to be created in 90 days. However, problems arise when trying to tie many disparate data marts together into an enterprise data mart. (Refer to the data warehouse versus data mart discussion in Chapter 4.)

Level 2

The mid-level data model contains the details, including the keys, attributes, subtypes, groupings, attributes, and connectors. For each high-level subject area identified, there is a single mid-level model. Do not put any thought into how the information will be retrieved or used. All that will come later. At this time, simply focus on the structure of the information—the attributes and the relationships between them as illustrated in Figure 5–3.

Because the data warehouse is developed one stage at a time (one mid-level model is transformed and readied for a data warehouse design, then another, and so forth), mid-level logical ERDs, including subject area keys, attributes, subtypes, and connectors, as well as the grouping of attributes, are built for each subject area.

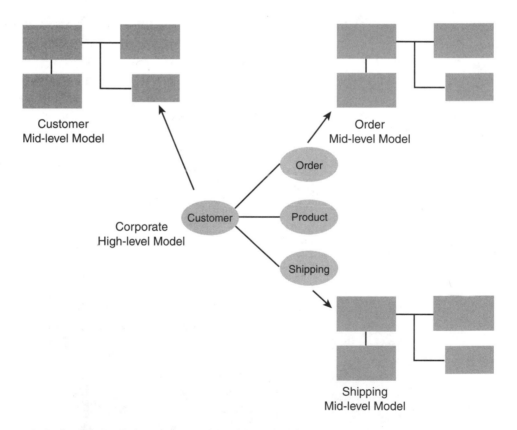

Figure 5–3 Each subject area has its own mid-level data model.

Entity—
A person, place, thing, or event about which the company records information. An entity is unique within the data model.

Relationship—
The business rule that associates two entities.

Key—
An element that uniquely identifies an entity.

Subtype—
The further logical division of an entity.

Connector—
The arrows between entities (indicate one-to-one, one-to-many, many-to-one, or many-to-many relationships).

Attribute—
The lowest level of information relating to an entity. It models one piece of information or a property of the entity (sometimes referred to as an element).

Level 3

After identifying your subject area (using the high-level subject area data model diagram you built and the interview results you gathered in the Planning & Analysis Phase), you are ready to create the third data warehouse dimensional data model. Levels 1, 2, and 4 of the model architecture have been discussed in OLTP ERD modeling for some time. Since data warehouses are focused on OLAP, we have added the concept of the data warehouse dimensional model, which represents information along multidimensional lines.

Before delving into creating the data warehouse/dimensional data model, remember to focus on the information first and the access paths second. In other words, don't focus on what the end-users do today because it will probably change. Also, trade off optimization for flexibility. Adaptability equals longer shelf life—it's worth trading off a little optimization for longevity.

After gathering the entity and relationship definitions, you can construct the normalized model. Generally speaking, the normalized, or 3rd Normal Form (3NF) model, is achieved when the attributes depend upon the key.

> 3rd Normal Form is an (non-key) attribute in which you remove all non-key dependencies on non-key columns. For example, if in an order table you have invoice_no, customer_no, customer_name, product_id, units, and amount, the customer_name needs to be removed because the customer_no is the key to the customer table which holds the customer_name and address information.

Characteristics of the normalized model include insensitivity to change—that is, making changes has a limited ripple effect on other areas. For example, if you change (add to or delete from) the attributes related to a particular key, you don't have to change other entities or relations. In this model, the retrieval paths for accessing information are very clear. On the other hand, performance can be awful. As such, *denormalizing* a data model is typically an attempt to improve performance. As a general rule, understand and enforce integrity constraints within a data warehouse. Integrity rules help guarantee the consistency of query results. However, enforcing integrity constraints may result in records being rejected during the load process.

Modeling Effort Scope

The modeling effort requires the following: accommodating the different levels of granularity; orienting the data to the major subjects; retaining only primitive data, and considering time variance. Obtaining the data will require: extracting the atomic-level data; loading the data into the departmental/individual level; enabling efficient and comprehensive access to the data; preserving historical integrity; and, structuring the data to meet evolving user requirements. If your organization does not have an enterprise wide data model, you can reverse-engineer subject area models from the physical data structures of candidate operational systems. Build the business logical model containing all of the major subject areas, but determine the detailed attributes for *only* the project subject areas.

The atomic level of the data warehouse should be designed to meet the informational requirements of the entire organization. As such, designing the physical data model requires balancing the goals and objectives of the current implementation with the overall information requirements of the organization.

Evolving the data warehouse data model into atomic-level physical data involves denormalizing the model, grouping data elements according to stability, and maintaining both detailed and derived data at the atomic level to meet different organizational requirements. (Note that atomic-level data is typically maintained in a relational database for better loading performance and modification flexibility.)

The atomic-level data in the data warehouse is the lowest level of data required to satisfy the business information requirements. Atomic-level data is not directly accessed by the end-users, but rather, it is used to summarize and calculate derivations that are then accessed directly. When determining atomic-level data accessibility, consider the amount of data, the number (and capabilities) of users, and the hardware, DBMS, and network performance requirements. Designed to facilitate loading efficiency, storage, and integrity, the atomic-level data model design is less focused on data access performance. (Note that the retention of atomic-level data usually involves a rolling summary. For example, keep transaction-level data for the most current 90 days, then summarize it for the next six months at the day level, the next year at the week level, the next three to five years at the month level, and so on.)

Department-level data is designed for optimal performance. Departmental-level data may be summarized, filtered, selected, denormalized, and/or derived from a lower level of detail. Generally, you store departmental data in OLAP form to provide analytical flexibility and accessibility to the data.

Identifying Data Sources

Data warehouse data comes from the operational environment, known as the *system of record*. Defining the system of record sets the stage for the mapping of data between the operational and data warehouse environments. When identifying the source system of record, the operational systems and other potential data sources are identified and analyzed, and the optimal sources are identified. Note that this activity is performed in parallel with determining and prioritizing the business requirements for information. The data modeler identifies each potential source system's technical environment and physical data characteristics. Overall stability and accessibility are also identified. Overall, the selection of the source system of record is based on data quality and characteristics, and the ability of the system to handle the data extraction and transport.

Data in the corporate data warehouse typically consists of: mainframe production data held in a hierarchical and network DBMS (it is estimated that 80% of corporate data is held in these types of DBMSs); departmental data held in proprietary file systems (VSAM, RMS) and RDBMSs (Informix, Oracle); and, private data held on workstations and servers. Making this data available within the warehouse involves extensive copy management, data replication, data summarization, and version control. And, the data warehouse must be available to the user, making critical the mechanisms for delivering data to the desktop, mining through different levels of data, and providing connectivity.

The data model provides the structure and content definition of the informational needs of the corporation. The data modeler takes the structure content designated by the operational mid-level business logical data model and uses that as a benchmark to locate the *best* data in a corporation. The *best* data is determined by what data is most accurate, most complete, most timely, best conforms to the structure specified by the data model, and is nearest to the originating source. Reviewing existing operational data models and data structures is typically undertaken only for the implementation subject area. In this activity, all entities of the candidate operational source systems are identified, and their relationships or linkages are defined and attributed. In this context, the operational data model represents the operational data in its *physical* storage architecture. When evaluating operational data models:

- Identify the keys and attributes of each entity in the model
- Ensure all attributes are sufficiently defined for future identification and analysis
- Identify repeating groups and data types
- Identify relationships between data groups
- Where possible, document domain values and distinguishing business rules

Note that there is no implication that the data ending up in the system of record is perfect, and defining the system of record has no impact on rebuilding the operational system. If some data is corrupt, initiate a separate project to correct the data.

Logic, algorithms, formatting, naming conventions, summarizations, and selection of records to be transformed define the mapping between the system of record and the data warehouse (see Chapter 8 for an illustration of meta data source to target mapping). Mapping conditions include:

- Default (the data warehouse must supply a default value where there is no operational data source)
- Attribute-to-attribute (when a source system attribute simply maps into another target data warehouse system attribute)
- Multiple attributes to single attribute (two systems map into one, and you must determine which is the appropriate source)
- Attribute->conversion->attribute (the attribute must be converted—restructuring formats, data types, logical conversion of codes, and algorithmic conversions—before it is placed in the warehouse)

When mapping data, consider the following: summarization (Will a single record be loaded or will many be summarized into one record and loaded?); frequency of transformation; data volume (affects how often records will be summarized and determines whether some or all records will be selected for entry into the warehouse); sorting sequence of the input file (Does the file need to be subsetted into smaller files for individual processing?); and, the identification of changes in the source system (see Figure 5–4). After defining the system of record and mapping the data, the data modeler should document, at a minimum:

- The attribute mapping between the operational system and data warehouse target
- The logic required to select and extract data from the source system
- The conversions required as data passes from the source to the target
- The frequency of transformation
- The volume of data to be transformed
- Whether the source data will be passed record-by-record or summarized

The sources of information residing in the data warehouse will cross vertical and horizontal business partitions; for example, finance, sales, and order processing will each have their own information technology budget and staff. It will prove to be a major challenge for organizations to obtain the necessary data access rights to source the data warehouse, making backing from high-level management imperative.

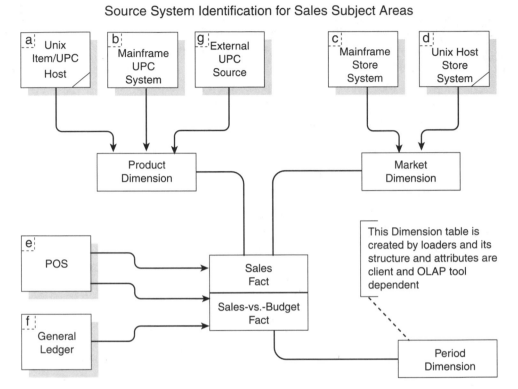

Figure 5–4 Mapping data sources.

Building the Dimensional Model

The dimensional model defines how the user will access information; it is similar to how the users *think* of the information. Building the dimensional model includes aggregating the data, choosing the grain, and choosing dimensions. Dimensional hierarchies can be represented:

- Vertically: Use when the aggregates are pre-constructed; drilling operations require one SQL statement per level.
- Horizontally: Use when all aggregates are calculated dynamically; drilling operations can be performed with a single join.
- Combined: Efficient for aggregated databases; supports multi-level drilling.

See Figure 5–5 for an example dimensional data model.

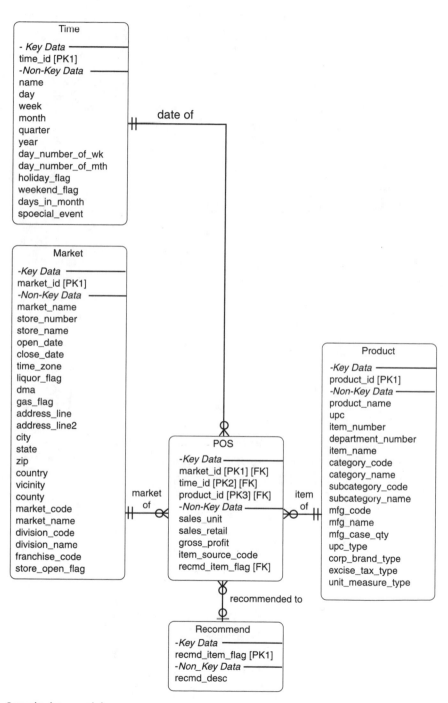

Figure 5–5 Sample data model.

You can implement hierarchies within your dimensions horizontally, vertically, or by using a combination. For example, if you were implementing your dimension horizontally, your table structure would look like Table 5–1.

Table 5–1 Horizontal Table Structure

time_id	time_name	day	week	month	years
1	07-06-1997	184	28	7	1997
2	07-7-1997	185	28	7	1997
3	07-08-1997	186	28	7	1997
4	07-09-1997	187	28	7	1997

A typical query tool (for example, Oracle Discover 2000, Business Objects, Brio Query, or Cognos Impromptu) can drill up or down based on a meta data table defining drill parentage rules (or hierarchy rules). Using the table above, *day* would be defined as having no columns for its *children* and *week* would be defined as its parent. *Week* would be defined as having *day* as its child and *month* as its parent. When drilling down via a front-end tool in week 26 of the current year, an SQL query would be generated to get all of the *time_id* rows where the week equals 26 and the year equals 1997. These seven rows would then be joined against the fact table to retrieve the applicable measures.

For performance reasons, a vertical query tool (for example, Information Advantage) adds additional rows to the table to represent the hierarchy (see an example of a time dimension table, Table 5–2). For example, your table structure would add an additional column (indicating level) and use it via the layout screen for selecting the time period on which to report. It would then represent this time period in an outline format. In the front-end tool content screen, you'd choose the time period you're interested in by drilling down on the year, month, week, and/or day to constrain your query measures. The front-end tool would use the level column to more quickly select the rows that make up the proper parentage.

Table 5–2 Vertical Table Structure

time_id	time_name	level	day	week	month	years
1	07-06-1997	day	184	28	7	1997
2	07-7-1997	day	185	28	7	1997
1,000	wb 02-09-97	week		28	7	1997
1,001	wb 02-10-97	week		28	7	1997
4,000	feb 97	month			2	1997

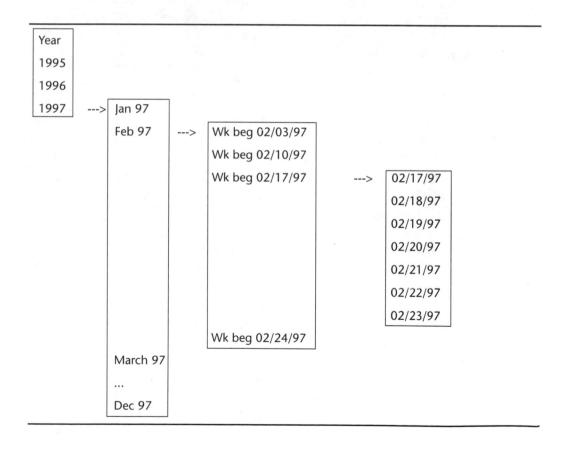

Because end-user queries can require the aggregation of hundreds or thousands of rows, *pre-aggregating* some or all of a data warehouse can dramatically reduce query response time. (Note that you'll trade pre-aggregation for more storage.) Consider dynamic aggregation if the fact table is large but structurally simple; consider pre-aggregation if the fact table is small but structurally complex. Pre-aggregation stores each set of aggregate information in a different fact table, or stores detailed and aggregate data in the same fact table. Typically, you pre-aggregate one or more dimensional structures when:

1. The compression ratio is low, when rows displayed are less than rows retrieved, resulting in longer retrieval time

> Compression ratio is the ratio of rows retrieved to rows displayed. For example, if you wanted to see **all products** as your product dimension constraint—all product rows in the table would be returned, but only one row, titled **all products**, would be displayed.

2. The dimensional structure is very complex (for example, a structure requiring several joins to traverse from the starting to the ending point in the dimension)

3. The computations are very complex (although the SQL to compute a particular fact is simple, it requires computing some prior fact, which requires computing some prior fact, and so on)

To determine whether or not to pre-aggregate a particular dimension, determine the compression factor for each level of the dimension. Divide the number of rows produced by an aggregation by the number of rows retrieved. For example, if we retrieved 900 rows and reported on 32 rows, the compression factor would be 32/900, or .035. Do not pre-aggregate dimensions having compression factors close to 1.0. A compression factor that is close to 1.0 will result in a dimension explosion—the size of the aggregates will be close in size to the original fact table. Note that facts depending upon numbers that are aggregated do not aggregate nor do inter-row calculations; however, these are usually simple (and therefore fast) SQL statements.

There is a need for both detailed data and summary data. But, massive amounts of detailed data hide significant trends and patterns and do not promote standardization of analysis. Also, the cost of both storage and processing is huge. On the other hand, many industries have discovered the value of detailed data. Summary data can lead to average data, which then leads to average decisions. Create summary tables: when usage dictates the need and DASD capacity allows it; for identification of long-term trends; for standardization; and, for better performance. Choosing the level of detail for a fact table is frequently referred to as *choosing the grain*—typically, in a data mart, the level of granularity is reflected at the weekly level. For example, transactions are summarized for each product at each location for the week.

Dimensions are used for browsing and launching constraint values. An end-user's report uses dimensions as row headers, making the data understandable. Data marts should only share dimensions if they are the same dimension or one is a mathematical subset of the other. Shared dimensions are referred to as *conformed*. A conformed dimension would be, for example, the *Customer* dimension. When dimensions are identified similarly across data marts, data marts can be built by different teams and then merged into the overall data warehouse. If the dimensions of two data marts are conformed, it is easy to implement drill-across by sending separate queries to the two data marts and then sort-merging the two answer sets on a set of common row headers.

Time is probably the most common dimension. For example, you can structure a calendar as fiscal or rolling. The *Time* dimension appears to be straightforward, but then you notice that two months (and quarters and years) can occur in the same week. You can name the weeks so that you split them in the middle (SepWk5 and OctWk1); or, you can define alternate rollups for weeks that also include the full five days. Or optimally, you can build separate hierarchies so that *day* is related to *week /month*.

Categorical dimensions are typically used in support of some analytical process and are related to an attribute (*recommended* versus *not recommended*) rather than to a primary key. Category analysis can be a very large performance drain on the system, however, because the dependency on an attribute (rather than an indexed foreign key) may require full-table scans for some queries. It is common for a categorical dimension to be used in many queries, especially if you have different aggregate fact tables. Whether you create categorical dimensions or leave the categorization process to a query depends upon the complexity of the categorization and how frequently it needs to be analyzed.

Do not confuse informational and partitioning dimensions. If you have a series of attributes that have column names like Actual Sales, Budget Sales, Forecast Sales, Actual Units, Budget Units, and Forecast Units, then have three partitions—Actual, Budget, and Forecast. The informational dimension contains only Sales and Units.

For example, my data warehouse implementation at a large retailer had five dimensions, including Product, Location, Period, Vendor, and Recommended. The Vendor and Time dimensions changed slowly; for example, a store may have been assigned to a different market or a business segment. To accommodate tracking changes in these slowly-changing dimensions, we could have:

1. Overwritten the old values in the dimension record (losing historical data)

2. Created an additional dimension record with the new attribute values, thus segmenting history accurately between the old description and new description

3. Created new fields within the original dimension record to record the new attribute values, keeping the original attribute values as well

We chose the second option because it enabled us to accurately track the history of changes. The first choice was the easiest to implement. And, the third choice was equipped to handle only two values of the changed attribute—the original and current values of the changed attribute. Intermediate values were lost and the history of changes couldn't be tracked effectively.

If a store was transferred from market X to market Y on July 21, 1997, the initial market X would apply to all fact records associated with the store up to July 21, 1997, and the new market Y would apply to all fact records on or after July 21, 1997. This is accomplished by creating an additional record for the store in the MARKET table with market set to Y. To identify and access the different versions of the records from the MARKET table, the primary key of the MARKET table needs to be changed from market_id to market_id followed by a version number. A three-digit serial or version number allows us to keep track of 1000 changes for a store, or 1000 snapshots of a particular store record. The store key stored in the fact table now is the new MARKET key, the market_id followed by the version number.

Chapter 6

DATAMAGIC:
DATABASE ADMINISTRATION

The database administrator is the data warehouse team member most likely to require some magic. First, the database administrator's deliverable is the physical database. Secondly, when implementation doesn't meet end-user expectations, the DBA is the first person they call—the one who must explain why queries take *too long* and reports take *too much time* to build—and the one who must undertake the mundane yet critical tasks like backing up ever-increasing amounts of data.

This chapter focuses on your critical responsibilities (capacity planning, designing, and building the physical model, and database administration) and gives some tips on how to accomplish these tasks—for those times when waving your wand and wishing for datamagic just isn't enough.

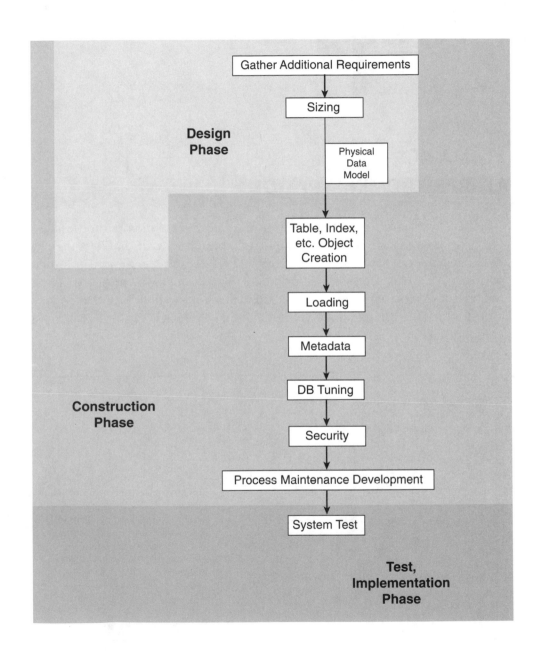

Decision support systems should work efficiently with other components of a larger system. They should be able to access broad sources of data and interface with the necessary system tools to make the available data easy to find and easy to understand. While a simple charting or reporting tool can be used to provide information on which to base a decision, there are more processes required. Data may have to be copied, manipulated, or enriched for it to be usable by the reporting tool. And after presentation, the information must be communicated to justify the decision. This is the whole process of decision support. It must be looked at from data to communication. The database administrator must understand and execute capacity planning, convert the logical data model to the physical model, assist in the DBMS platform selection, assist in the creation and management of meta data, install and support the OLAP analysis tool, perform ongoing performance tuning, assist in the data loading, and manage security.

This chapter first focuses on capacity planning for both disk and processor. It then discusses primary administration tasks, including performance tuning, security, and creating and loading the data warehouse. Finally, we highlight the steps required to design and build the physical model.

See Chapter 4 for a discussion of DBMSs.

Capacity Planning

Capacity planning in the data warehouse centers around planning disk storage and processing resources. There is an important but indirect relationship between data and processing power—the more data, the more processing power required.

> **Disk storage capacity** encompasses the level of detail stored, the length of time data is kept, and the number of occurrences of data to be stored. **Processor capacity** refers to the environment workload. **Workload** encompasses background processing and predictable /unpredicatable end-user access.

Given the volume of data and type of processing that goes against the data, the data warehouse is capable of consuming large amounts of resources. For organizations wanting to be proactive—that is, they don't want to be surprised by hardware resource utilization and prefer to anticipate system response time prior to building the system—capacity planning for the data warehouse environment is critical.

Capacity planning for the data warehouse is tricky because: 1) the workload is variable; and 2) the volume of data is far greater than that encountered in the operational environment. Data volume is determined by granularity—the finer the degree of granularity, the more data and disk storage required.

When considering data *storage*, determine: the DBMS' capabilities and efficiencies (how much data the DBMS will handle); how the data will be stored, compressed, indexed, and encoded; whether locking will be suppressed; whether requests will be monitored based on resource utilization; whether data will be physically denormalized; whether data will be partitioned and accessed in parallel; and, the support that will be provided for the meta data. When determining the *capacity* required for your data warehouse, consider data volume, hardware platform, disk storage, and network software. Your capacity estimate should include factors for retention, summarization, managed redundancy, indexes, data staging, backups, archiving, system software, application software, RDBMS software, end-user software, mirroring, recovery, sort temp work areas, and database and tool maintenance work areas.

All sizes, estimates, and assumptions should be liberal, since data warehouse capacity expands exponentially. Consider calculating current and 12-24 month estimates. The initial business requirements for information identified by end-users will probably result in an unrealistic volume and/or granularity of data. Identify the cost and implications of satisfying these requirements and then discuss the results with the data warehouse team and end-users regarding realistic and achievable volumes of data to be captured, processed, and stored.

Disk Storage Capacity

Calculating required disk storage capacity is straightforward:

- Identify the very large fact tables
- Calculate how may rows there will be in each table (the answer to this question depends on the granularity; the lower the level of detail, the more rows required)
- Calculate the row size (estimate the contents of each row—keys *and* attributes)
- Factor in the needed indexes

Often, hardware and software make up the largest cost components of a data warehouse implementation. Hardware requirements are driven by the data volume which, in turn, is driven by the business requirements for historical data and the level of granularity. To estimate data volume:

- Calculate the record size for each table
- Estimate the number of initial records for each table
- Review the data warehouse access requirements (to predict index requirements)
- Determine the growth factor for each table
- Identify the largest target table expected over the selected period of time and add approximately 25-30% overhead to the table size to determine temporary storage size

The estimation of table and index storage can then be added to the other storage requirements as follows:

1. Target table index size = (SUM [1 to n] field length(n) + 10), where *n* is an indexed field

2. Target table size = (largest number of rows * rows length + index size) * retention factor * growth factor

3. Data warehouse size = (SUM 1 to t) table size(t) + staging area + software + development + test + DASD mirroring, where *t* is each target table

(Note that if the actual is 80-100% of the estimate, the estimate was successful.)

Table 6–1 is a sample disk storage sizing estimate for a company in the retail industry.

Table 6–1 Sample Disk Storage Sizing Estimate

Object Name	Type	# Rows	Size	Row Initial	Notes
POS	Table	1,200,000,000	72	6,400,000,000	Store/day/item granularity. Assumes 6,000 stores/500 items sold per store per day for 400 days.
Product	Table	100,000	300	30,000,000	Recommended/non-recommended.
Market	Table	6,000	368	2,208,000	

Table 6–1 Sample Disk Storage Sizing Estimate *(continued)*

Object Name	Type	# Rows	Size	Row Initial	Notes
Time	Table	1,825	35	63,875	Holds 5 years of time data.
POS Load	Table	500,000	97	48,500,000	Temporary table used to load POS.
POS PK	Index	1,200,000,000	27	32,400,000,000	
Product PK	Index	100,000	14	1,400,000	
Market PK	Index	6,000	6	36,000	
Time PK	Index	1,825	7	2,775	
Prod N1	Index	100,000	30	3,000,000	Sub-category name; non-unique index for query.
Prod N2	Index	100,000	30	3,000,000	Category name; non-unique for query.
Prod N4	Index	100,000	14	1,400,000	Item Number.
Prod U1	Index	100,000	13	1,300,000	UPC Number; unique constraint for load.
Mkt N1	Index	6,000	30	180,000	Market Name.
Mkt N2	Index	6,000	30	180,000	Division Name.
Time N1	Index	1,825	100	182,500	Time Period Name.
Summary Tables	Table			1,000,000,000	Summary tables not yet defined.
System	Tspace	100,000,000		100,000,000	System table space required for Oracle.
Temporary	Tspace	2,000,000,000		2,000,000,000	Temporary table space for sorting and memory swap.
Rollback	Tspace	1,000,000,000		1,000,000,000	Rollback table space required for instance recovery and transaction consistency on batch loads.

Table 6–1 Sample Disk Storage Sizing Estimate *(continued)*

Object Name	Type	# Rows	Size	Row Initial	Notes
Oracle Code	Code	500,000,000		500,000,000	Oracle code, DBA reports, alert log, and trace files.
Archive Logging	Archive	2,000,000,000		2,000,000,000	Require archiving logging to be used because we will not be able to take the database down to do backups.
Overhead				50,000,000,000	To handle block headers, pctfree, pctused.
Other Tools	Tools			200,000,000	SQL*Lab; performance monitor tool(s).
Daily Data Files				50,000,000,000	FTP extraction files, load files.

Mid-1998 ObjectName	Months: 12 Size			Initial	Notes
POS	72			24,000,000,000	600 items per store per day.
Others				30,000,000,000	All other tables except summary tables, and all indexes.
Summary Tables				40,000,000,000	Summary tables.

Processor Capacity

Now, determine processing requirements for background, predictable DSS, and unpredictable DSS processing. *Background processing* is usually done in batch mode for extracting, loading, sorting, merging, scrubbing, cleansing, restructuring, aggregating, and indexing. Background processing can be run at off-peak times and can be spread out to fit the batch update window. *Predictable DSS processing* is done regularly, usually on a query or transaction basis. For both background and predictable processing, DBAs need to consider:

- Number of times a process will be run
- Number of I/Os a process will use
- Expected response time

Determine these factors by examining the pattern of calls made to the DBMS, as well as interaction with the operating system.

The critical performance benchmark occurs when the end-users are accessing the database (7am-7pm) rather than during batch updates, which usually occur at night or during the weekend. Create a workload matrix (or a profile of the processing workload), which is an intersection of the tables in the data warehouse and the processes (background, predictable) that will run in the data warehouse. Fill in the number of calls and resulting I/Os for an eight-hour period. The number of I/Os will depend on the number of rows in the block, whether a block is in memory when it's requested, the amount of buffers available, traffic, the DBMS, and indexing.

Now, create the actual workload profile. Each row in the matrix must be multiplied by the number of times it will execute in a day. At the bottom of the page, the totals must be calculated to reach an eight-hour I/O requirement. Next, calculate the hourly requirement. After calculating the hourly requirement, identify the peak system load. Then, determine the requirements for unpredictable requests and merge these with the high-water mark. Finally, factor in 10% for slack processing. Use this calculation to determine the MIPS required. Then, use this MIPs figure to determine which hardware vendor best fits your needs.

You'll also need to determine backup and mirroring requirements (more information on backup and mirroring is included in the following section)—plans for an off-line archive can ease data warehouse growth, while mirroring requirements can nearly double its anticipated size.

Database Administration

Part of the DBA's responsibilities include the following administration tasks:

- Capacity planning
- Monitoring usage and growth
- Assisting in the DBMS platform selection
- Assisting in the creation and management of meta data
- Supporting the OLAP environment (helps select and install the access/ analysis tool)
- Performing ongoing performance tuning
- Assisting in or performing data loading
- Managing security

Administrative tasks required when building the physical model include (among others):

- Setting up read-only table spaces
- Sizing temporary table spaces
- Determining whether to use archive logging mode
- Implementing hot or cold backups

DBAs work hard to maximize database and server performance—searching for new tuning parameters, better ways to balance I/O loads across server drives, and more efficient techniques to manage memory caches. DBAs also monitor application performance, ensure efficient SQL coding/database access, and identify problem SQL statements.

Performance Tuning

Obstacles to good performance are massive amounts of data, the diverse and unpredictable community of users, and the unpredictable patterns of utilization. But, multiple techniques are available for improving data warehouse performance. For example, basic performance tuning considerations could include:

- Replacing textual keys with numeric keys to decrease storage required for both data and indexes, thus increasing index access
- Denormalizing dimension tables to decrease the number of joins, thus improving access and performance
- Using a higher summary level or higher level of granularity than the lowest level of detail

Because the OLTP environment serves the immediate needs of the business, performance is critical—required transaction speeds hover around two to three seconds per transaction. On the other hand, the OLAP community is managerial, serving the planning and strategical needs of the business. OLAP performance refers to the length of time from the submission of a query or request by a user until the results of the query or the request are known. Performance enhancements in the OLAP can be approached via strategic, tactical, and/or operational means.

Strategic techniques to enhance performance include operating on data at other than the lowest levels of granularity. For example, tremendous performance gains are possible by operating on summary data. This approach is the least expensive cost-wise—no parallel hardware or specialized DMBS software is needed. Another strategic technique for performance improvement is that of doing analysis against a subset of detailed data or a sample. (Note, however, that this technique should be used only for statistical analysis.)

Another strategic technique is the creation and maintenance of meta data. Meta data provides a record of what has already been calculated at the summary level. By using this record, you can avoid recreating calculations, thus saving system resources. Meta data also saves system resources by providing a roadmap as to what data is present or absent in the data warehouse, negating the need for trial-and-error searching.

A third strategic technique for enhancing performance is taking advantage of both parallel hardware and parallel DBMSs (discussed in Chapter 4). For example, Oracle 7.3's parallel query performs the following in parallel: table scans, sorts, queries with distinct values, data loading, table creation (summary tables), building indexes, and recovery. See Table 6–2 for an example of creating a table with parallel degree 4. To utilize the Oracle 7.3 parallel query, set the following `init.ora` parameters:

```
parallel_default_max_instances
parallel_max_servers
parallel_min_percent
parallel_min_servers
parallel_server_idle_time
recovery_parallelism
```

Tactical techniques include the *star join* pioneered by Ralph Kimball. A star join is a data structure in which the bulk of the data is organized into fact tables. The fact tables contain data occurrences stored along with dimension tables, which contain less populous data that provides ancillary information about the fact tables. The star join is useful because the data needed for analysis—the facts—is conveniently organized for analysis, therefore negating the need to join fact data with lots of other data. For example, Oracle 7.3's optimizer recognizes a star schema. When using Oracle's optimizer, remember to collect statistics (histograms) after each batch of data is loaded.

Building summary aggregates of frequently accessed data is the best *tactical* technique for improving performance. For example, if you create a market summary fact table which calculates a store's (in a particular market) sales for each product during a specific time period, users can use this particular table for information rather than dynamically querying the lower level store table. Note that query monitoring software is available, enabling you to determine what aggregate tables need to be built.

The cost comparison for dynamic aggregation versus pre-aggregation depends upon how often levels of detail are requested. If the same question is asked twice, the second time that it's asked, pre-aggregation starts paying for itself. But, total pre-aggregation requires weighing the cost of calculating every aggregate versus calculating some aggregates more than once. Also, consider the *personnel* cost of waiting for large aggregations. Pre-aggregation makes sense if personnel *waiting* time is high enough and you're able to calculate the aggregates in a small off-line window.

Other tactical approaches to improving performance include:

- PREJOINS—Prejoining data to enhance performance; prejoins are done during off-hours
- ARRAYS—Creating and using arrays can result in enormous resource savings because they are located on or near the same physical block (For example, finding all of the months for an account may cost as little as one I/O. But, if the months are scattered around the database in a random normalized fashion, then finding every entry is burdensome.)
- CLUSTERING—Clustering is the technique of causing different units of data to be physically placed and managed in the same block of data as other related units (Note that this is DBMS-dependent.)
- COMPACTION—Data physically compacted when written into storage enables more data to be loaded into a block and the amount of data accessed upon retrieval to be optimized; optimum in the data warehouse because the environment operates in a non-updated mode
- MERGING TABLES—Merging tables lessens I/O being consumed upon the access of the data
- SELECTIVE REDUNDANCY— By introducing selective redundancy into the equation, the system designer can maximize access
- ROLLING SUMMARY DATA—Keeping new detailed data to age into higher levels of summarization (For example, hourly data may be kept for today's activities; daily data may be kept for each day of this week's activities; and, weekly weekly data may be kept for this month's. As time passes, data are summarized into successively higher levels. The creation of rolling summary structures is especially applicable to the data warehouse because both detailed and summarized levels are needed.)

For example, Oracle 7.3 uses hash joins to improve performance. (Note that an SQL join involves joining two or more tables' data to answer a query. When tables are joined, the DBMS constructs a number of dynamic, temporary tables to manage the data sort. Oracle uses disk and memory to store the temporary tables.) The hash join in Oracle 7.3 is an in-memory hash table built on-the-fly as the query is processed, significantly increasing performance. To implement hash joins, set three new `init.ora` parameters:

```
1. hash_join_enabled=TRUE
2. hash_area_size=(default is twice the sort_area_size)
3. hash_multiblock_to_count set high
```

Operational approaches include:

- Using the DBMS load utility
- Dropping creation of indexes at the moment of load; recreating indexes after the load
- Purging the data warehouse frequently; removing unwanted and unnecessary data to streamline other processing
- Enabling *charge-back*s to remind the organization that resources consumed by the DSS analyst aren't free

In addition, by adding bit-mapped indices to low-cardinality, frequently-searched fields, you can improve performance and lessen storage requirements.

> **Cardinality** is a measurement of the number of unique values in a column in a table compared to the total number of rows in the table. Low is less than 5%

A bit-mapped index creates an array where the columns are the domain of the key and the rows correspond to rows of the table. Each value in the array is an on/off bit that indicates whether that row is pointed to by that index. The bit-map index will save considerable storage space as compared to the btree index.

> **Bit-mapped indexes** indicate the existence or nonexistence of a condition. Bit-mapped indexes are good for data warehouses because they require minimal storage and are structured for queries. However, they are not effective for updates because each row in the index table must be reviewed prior to updating the table. (We recommend dropping the indexes prior to a batch load and recreating them after the load.)

If you're using Oracle's DBMS, you can make additional operational performance enhancements by using:

- Read-only tablespaces (`[alter tablespace table_name read only;]`)
- Partitioned views
- No redo logs (`create ... unrecoverable`)
- Miscellaneous `init.ora` parameters (`db_file_multiblock_read_count` , `sort_area_size`)

Security

The data warehouse is built for data access—for example, the data warehouse is considered a failure if it cannot accommodate easy and unconstrained access. Ironically, security of data in the data warehouse requires that data access be limited and controlled. However, once operational data is transformed and placed in the data warehouse, data is available for one and all to use.

Most DBMSs offer security features. A simple disk dump that accesses and offloads data at the physical block level is totally available and deciphered—making it insecure. Also, the data warehouse is a tempting target for unauthorized access because of the lengthy storage period. Because it is easy to bypass typical DBMS security features, the only effective approach to securing data is to encrypt the data at the moment of writing. (Usually, only non-keyed, non-indexed data is encoded.) Don't forget that encoded data must be decoded upon front-end access. Using a decoding routine, audit trails can be created; when someone accesses the data warehouse and calls the decoding routine, you're able to monitor who is logging in. Finally, determine if you're going to use the front-end access tool security, the DBMS' security, or a combination of the two. For example, in Oracle, you would use roles and/or views for security.

Creating and Loading the Data Warehouse

See Figures 6-1, 6-2, and 6-3 for examples of creating database objects and preparing the database for loading. (See Chapter 7 for additional information about loading.) We recommend implementing a staging area for scrubbing, cleansing, and validating incremental batch-loaded data prior to updating the data in the data warehouse schema. This shortens data warehouse downtime, thereby increasing end-user access time.

Designing and Building the Physical Model

A good physical model is often the difference between data warehouse success and failure. The design of the physical model builds on the logical model with the addition of indexes, referential integrity, and physical storage characteristics (for example, initial extent, percent increase, degree of parallelism, and storage placement). See Figures 6-1, 6-2, and 6-3 for a sample DDL.

> **DDL** (data definition language) refers to (among others) the **create index**, **create table**, **create tablespace**, and **grant access** commands that prepare your schema for loading.

Transforming the logical data model into the physical model includes:

- Adding indexes (primary, unique, non-unique, and bit-mapped) for load programs and end-user access; may include dropping and recreating before and after batch load routines (see Figure 6–1)
- Adding referential integrity constraints (foreign key and primary key relationships) (see Figure 6–2)
- Determining where to place database objects on disk (disk mapping, striping, or RAID—if using RAID, then determining the configuration strategy and what to mirror)
- Defining storage parameters for database objects (see Table 6-2—this example is Oracle-dependent)
- Setting initialization parameters for size, scope, access, and joins (see Table 6–3)
- Implementing the star schema design (segmenting *too large* fact tables vertically or horizontally)
- If joins are excessive, further denormalizing dimension tables
- Adding fields for audit ability (for example, last load/updated date)
- Utilizing parallel processing (see the **Parameters** column in Table 6–2)
- Adding check constraints (see Figure 6–3)

```
CREATE INDEX PERIOD_N1 ON PERIOD
( PERIOD_DATE )
  PCTFREE 1
  TABLESPACE IDX
  STORAGE (
    INITIAL 256K
    NEXT 256K
    PCTINCREASE 0 )
  UNRECOVERABLE;

CREATE BITMAP INDEX POS_N2 ON POS
( PERIOD_ID )
  PCTFREE 1
  TABLESPACE IDX
  STORAGE (
    INITIAL 16M
    NEXT 4M
    PCTINCREASE 0 )
  UNRECOVERABLE
  PARALLEL (DEGREE 4);

CREATE BITMAP INDEX POS_N1 ON POS
( MARKET_ID )
  PCTFREE 1
  TABLESPACE IDX
  STORAGE (
    INITIAL 16M
    NEXT 4M
    PCTINCREASE 0 )
  UNRECOVERABLE
  PARALLEL (DEGREE 4);

CREATE BITMAP INDEX POS_N3 ON POS
( PRODUCT_ID )
  PCTFREE 1
  TABLESPACE IDX
  STORAGE (
    INITIAL 16M
    NEXT 4M
    PCTINCREASE 0 )
  UNRECOVERABLE
  PARALLEL (DEGREE 4)
```

Figure 6–1 An example of Oracle's `create index` DDL

ALTER TABLE POS
  ADD (CONSTRAINT POS_MARKET_FK
    FOREIGN KEY (MARKET_ID)
      REFERENCES MARKET) ;

ALTER TABLE POS
  ADD (CONSTRAINT POS_PERIOD_FK
    FOREIGN KEY (PERIOD_ID)
      REFERENCES PERIOD) ;

ALTER TABLE POS
  ADD (CONSTRAINT POS_PRODUCT_FK
    FOREIGN KEY (PRODUCT_ID)
      REFERENCES PRODUCT) ;

Figure 6–2 An example of Oracle's referential integrity constraints.

Table 6–2 Table Storage Parameters

Table Name	Physical Parameters
POS	PCTFREE 10 PCTUSED 80 TABLESPACE STAGING_Tbl STORAGE (INITIAL 64M NEXT 16M PCTINCREASE 0) PARALLEL (DEGREE 4)
POS_LOAD	PCTFREE 10 PCTUSED 80 TABLESPACE STAGING_Tbl STORAGE (INITIAL 64M NEXT 16M PCTINCREASE 0) PARALLEL (DEGREE 4)
PRODUCT	PCTFREE 20 PCTUSED 70 TABLESPACE STAGING_Tbl STORAGE (INITIAL 16M NEXT 4M PCTINCREASE 0) PARALLEL (DEGREE 4)
MARKET	PCTFREE 10 PCTUSED 80 TABLESPACE STAGING_Tbl STORAGE (INITIAL 1M NEXT 1M PCTINCREASE 0) PARALLEL (DEGREE 4)
TIME	PCTFREE 0 PCTUSED 100 TABLESPACE STAGING_Tbl STORAGE (INITIAL 1M NEXT 1M PCTINCREASE 0) PARALLEL (DEGREE 4)

Table 6–3 Database Initialization Parameters

Parameter	PDS1	PDSA
alway_anti_join	HASH	HASH
audit_file_dest	?/rdbms/audit	?/rdbms/audit
audit_trail	NONE	NONE
checkpoint_process	TRUE	TRUE
compatible	7.3.2.3.0	7.3.2.3.0
cpu_count	4	4
cursor_space_for_time	TRUE	TRUE
db_block_buffers	16,000	8,000
db_block_checkpoint_batch	4	8
db_block_lru_latches	4	4
db_block_size	16,384	8,192
db_file_multiblock_read_count	4	8
db_file_simultaneous_writes	4	8
db_writers	1	1
dml_locks	1,000	1,000
enqueue_resources	1,000	1,000
hash_area_size	65,536	65,536
hash_join_enabled	TRUE	TRUE
hash_multiblock_io_count	4	8
log_archive_buffers	4	4
log_archive_buffer_size	64	64
log_buffer	4,194,304	4,194,304
log_checkpoint_interval	1,000,000	1,000,000
log_checkpoint_timeout	0	0

Table 6–3 Database Initialization Parameters *(continued)*

log_simultaneous_copies	8	8
open_cursors	1,000	1,000
open_links	8	8
optimizer_percent_parallel	100	100
parallel_min_servers	4	4
parallel_max_servers	32	32
parallel_server_idle_time	10	10
partition_view_enabled	TRUE	TRUE
sequence_cache_entries	100	1,000
share_pool_size	104,857,600	52,428,800
sort_area_size	65,536	65,536
sort_area_retained_size	65,536	65,536
sort_direct_writes	TRUE	TRUE
sort_write_buffers	4	4
sort_write_buffer_size	65,536	65,536
use_async_io	TRUE	TRUE

```
CREATE TABLE POS (
   MARKET_ID       NUMBER(7) NOT NULL,
   PERIOD_ID       NUMBER(7) NOT NULL,
   PRODUCT_ID      NUMBER(7) NOT NULL,
   RECMD_FLAG      CHAR(1) NOT NULL
         CONSTRAINT YES_NO10   CHECK (RECMD_FLAG IN ('N', 'Y')),
   NEW_ITEM_FLAG   CHAR(1) NOT NULL
         CONSTRAINT YES_NO11   CHECK (NEW_ITEM_FLAG IN ('N', 'Y')),
   SALES_UNIT      NUMBER(7,2) NULL,
   SALES_RETAIL    NUMBER(7,2) NULL,
   SALES_COST      NUMBER(7,2) NULL
)
   PCTFREE 10
   PCTUSED 80
   TABLESPACE DSS_Tbl
   STORAGE (
     INITIAL 64M
     NEXT 16M
     PCTINCREASE 0
   ) ;

ALTER TABLE POS
   ADD ( CONSTRAINT POS_PK PRIMARY KEY (MARKET_ID, PERIOD_ID,
PRODUCT_ID)
   USING INDEX
     PCTFREE 1
     TABLESPACE IDX
     STORAGE (
       INITIAL 16M
       NEXT 4M
       PCTINCREASE 0
   ) ) ;
```

Figure 6–3 An example of a check constraint within Oracle's create table DDL.

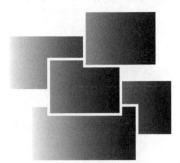

Chapter 7

_?_ CHANGES EVERYTHING:
A. EXTRACTION
B. TRANSFORMATION
C. SCRUBBING

Data extraction actually includes triggering, filtering, extracting, transforming, integrating, cleaning, and loading data from the legacy systems of record into the data warehouse. Data extraction ranges from simple extracts and loads to complex captures of changed data and updates to the data warehouse.

Extracting data refers to the process and tools that support transformation, summarization, and cleansing of data when moving data from one location to the data warehouse.

159

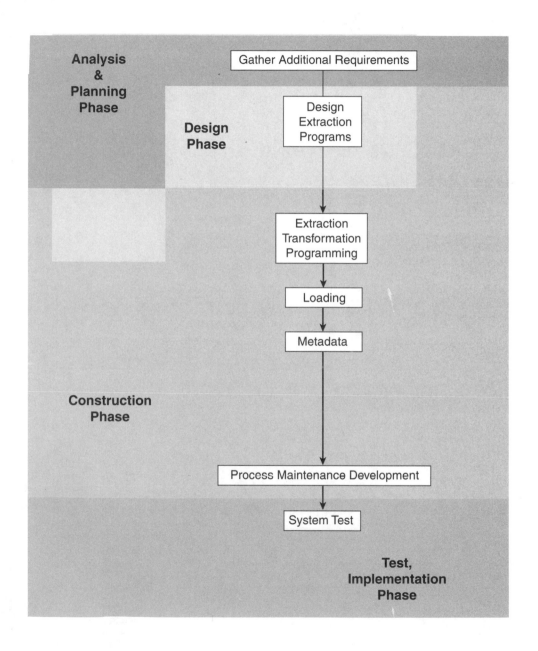

This chapter highlights the process that enables you to transform data into information and discusses the tools required for cleansing, summarizing, and aggregating source data before placing it in the data warehouse. We first discuss extraction, transformation, and scrubbing requirements and tools, followed by a review of the data loading and post-data loading processes. We include a program function specification and data flow diagram examples to load and transform the data.

Extraction, Transformation, & Scrubbing Tools

Extraction, transformation, and scrubbing tools enable data movement and data transformation into a secondary data source, which then can be accessed directly by users. Data extract tools and batch extract routines are particularly beneficial for moving a non-SQL database into an SQL DBMS. Extracting data from one location into the data warehouse requires:

- Data retrieval—The extraction of data from heterogeneous, operational databases
- Consolidation—The merging of various data sets into a master data set (involves standardizing data types and fields)
- Scrubbing—The cleaning of data to remove any inconsistencies or inaccuracies
- Summarizing—The data resulting from the retrieval, consolidation, and scrubbing process must be summarized to obtain reasonable query response times
- Updating the meta data repository—The repository should be kept up-to-date with any new data definitions; the meta data should be current and consistent
- Allowing for periodic or trickle feed update—The data in the warehouse will quickly become out-of-date if new operational data is not added at regular intervals
- If applicable, loading of the initial history

See Chapter 4 for a discussion of extraction, transformation, and scrubbing tools. We recommend purchasing a tool to decrease the potential of human error resulting from manual coding, to shorten the time required to complete the task, and to generate task documentation automatically.

Use a database gateway or data extraction tool (for example, Prism Warehouse Manager) to perform the complex process of extracting, transforming, and integrating data from across heterogeneous data sources to the data warehouse. Transformation engines (TEs) are an emerging technology that also assist in this process by providing strong data integration and transformation capabilities. TE vendors include:

- Apertus Technologies (Enterprise Integrator)
- Informatica (PowerMart Suite)[1]
- Reliant Data Systems (Data Conversion Language Engine)
- The SQL Group (Information Junction)

Transformation engines reduce the complexity of data integration while providing a multitasking technology architecture which performs transformation functions in parallel (leveraging your parallel hardware and DBMS by deploying the engine on a separate processor from both the production system and data warehouse, providing greater performance and throughput). You can define tasks to perform various functions (for example, data cleansing) at scheduled times or event intervals. When used with changed data capture technology (for example, IBM's Data Propagator products), you can *drip feed* data to the data warehouse on an ongoing basis instead of undertaking massive uploads. For organizations already using homegrown extraction applications, TEs can augment and/or replace these applications and the complex logic required for integration (reducing support and maintenance costs).

TEs focus primarily on complex data integration and transformation capabilities and not on obtaining data from operational sources. You'll have to determine the best way to deliver data to the TE. However, TEs enable complex integration and transformation and improved support for the operational data store, as well as the ability the handle data feeds concurrently from multiple points.

Data Loading

After completing the following data extraction steps, you'll be ready to load the data. But first:

- Identify the required fields from the source system
- Provide detailed descriptions of the transformations to the fields
- Identify triggering events that will result in extraction
- Create the process flows depicting the optimal extraction approach

1. See the discussion of Informatica's PowerMart Suite in Chapter 4.

Then, you're ready to load the data. There are three types of data loads:

1. Loading data already archived.
2. Loading data contained in existing applications.
3. Loading changes from the previous data load.

Loading data *already archived* is the simplest type of load because it's typically done once, and there is a minimal amount of concern as to the resources consumed by the loading of archival data. It does, however, require a custom program for each new source of input.

Loading *existing application* data requires a conversion from the operational DBMS to the data warehouse DBMS. Conversion methods include:

1. Exporting the existing system's database to a sequential flat file and performing the transformation of data into the data warehouse using the flat files (or, export the file, ftp the file to the data warehouse server, and then import the file using your data warehouse DBMS utility).

2. Creating extraction program specifications (write and debug code), transferring the file to the server, and creating a second program function specification to load and transform the data (see Figure 7–1 for an example of a program function specification to load TIME_DIM_TBL, and see Figure 7–2 which depicts the data flow program logic).

3. Using an off-the-shelf package (Carleton, Prism, or Evolutionary) to design the extraction via the program's 4GL GUI (note that this method has the added benefit of capturing the meta data automatically for source-to-target mappings), moving the file to the data warehouse server, and using the GUI for load and post-load processing.

When refreshing data *changed from the previous data load*, you must identify changes since the last time the data warehouse was refreshed. You can:

- Replace an entire table
- Use dates in the operational source to select only the appropriate records
- Use an operational source-created delta or audit file
- Trap changes at the DBMS level
- Compare a *before* image to an *after* image (frequently used since OLTP logs that trap changes can be disabled, thus losing any changes)

For example, the Oracle SQL Loader parallelization feature (which Oracle claims can load over 100GB per hour when using the parallel and direct path load options) allows multiple processes to load data into the same table at the same time. The SQL Loader direct path option allows SQL Loader to bypass the usual background database write processes (utilizing less resources) and directly load data from memory to the database table. You could use the following to load two source files into the same table in parallel:

```
>sqlldr userid=user/passwd control=market1.ctl direct=true
    parallel=true
>sqlldr userid=user/passwd control=market2.ctl direct=true
    parallel=true
```

Oracle's Transparent Gateways tool assists in data transformation and loading by accessing non-Oracle databases with Oracle SQL as if the data resided in an Oracle database. (If you're using Oracle->Oracle, just set up Oracle links.) Transparent Gateways also permits summarization, data derivation, and changing data types as they're moved into Oracle. More complex data transformations can be performed by first placing the data into a staging area, and then performing standard PL/SQL logic to clean, scrub, and transform the data as you move it to the final data warehouse table.

Post-load Processes

Post-load processes include:

- Data cleansing (may or may not be implemented at the time of extraction; it may be necessary to wait until the data is loaded into a staging area for the atomic level data cleansing to be performed—see Chapter 6 for more information on staging areas).
- Referential integrity verification (of the newly loaded atomic level data)
- Updating atomic-level summary data (from detailed data accumulated over a period of time)
- Creation and maintenance of system-generated primary (sequence generators) keys with the DBA
- Identification of orphan child records and other error correction activities

Subsequent data acquisition occurs between the atomic level of the data warehouse and the departmental level. During this activity, create a detailed set of requirements for each atomic level data acquisition process identifying:

- Input file characteristics
- Data cleansing approach

- Simple transformations
- Business rules
- Complex transformations (table look-ups)
- Pre-load derivation algorithms
- Insert or update approach
- Triggering events in the system of record identifying when the extracts should occur (timing)
- Filters applied to ensure that only the appropriate data is extracted
- Pre-load transformation and integration

When data quality problems occur during the extraction process (for example, *reject errors* and *do not load* errors are logged in the exception log), you can accept the error(s) and continue the load, correct the error(s) during the load process, and/or apply a default when loading bad data. (See the create table syntax for creating a summary table with the unrecoverable Oracle 7.3 option included in Chapter 6.)

Program Function Specification and Data Flow Diagram Examples

The following is an example of an extraction program specification which requires creating the program specification (write and debug code), transferring the file to the server, and creating a second program function specification to load and transform the data. Table 7–1 is an example of a program function specification to load TIME_DIM_TBL and Figure 7–1 depicts the data flow program logic.

Table 7–1 Load Time Dimension program function specification

Load Time Dimension Program Function	Specification
Program Identification:	loadtimedim
Program / Function Long Name:	Load Time Dimension Table
Functional Description:	Creates one row in time table for each day, for a period of five years
Performance Requirements:	NA
Name of Program Shell To Be Used:	loadtimedim.sh
Input Parameters:	start date (DD-MM-YY) number of years (defaults to 5)
Static Variables:	none

Table 7–1 Load Time Dimension program function specification *(continued)*

Load Time Dimension Program Function	Specification
Database / File Information	
File(s):	none
Table(s): TIME_DIM_TBL	
Access Type:	INSERT
Include Members:	NA
Output / Return Parameters:	none
Screen / Window Name:	none
Report Information:	none
Switches:	none
Internal Tables:	NA
Called by:	NA
Called Programs:	NA
Return Codes:	0–successful
	1–failed (see log file)

Program Functions (in outline form)

Use SQL*Plus to execute a PL/SQL block which:

     1. Deletes existing rows, if any, from TIME_DIM_TBL.

     2. For start_date to (number_of_years from start_date) loops:

       –assign values to day, week, and mth using to_char() function
       –compute fiscal_period
       –look up HOLIDAYS_TBL for holiday_flag and special_event
       –end loop.

     3. Commits changes.

Describe Processing/Editing/Calculations

Comparable day last year is the same day of the same week number last year. For example, the comparable day last year for Tuesday, 2/4/97 is Tuesday, 2/6/96. They both belong to week #6 of their respective years. Weeks are defined for this table as Monday through Sunday.

Table 7–1 Load Time Dimension program function specification *(continued)*

Testing Requirements

1. Choose and save a specific date range, five years long, for regression testing.
2. Save record count, number of work days, number of holidays, etc. for later comparison.
3. Provide instruction for running tests.

For each instance of error, at least one error message must be logged in the application log file.

Error	Action
Any kind of database error	Abend
Holidays not yet defined for specified date range	Warning

**When program abends, all changes made to TIME_DIM_TBL need to be rolled back.

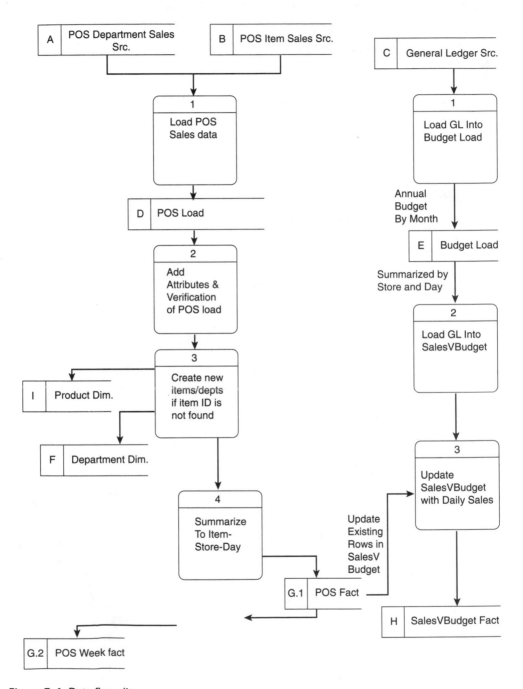

Figure 7–1 Data flow diagram.

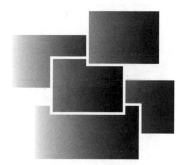

Chapter 8

Digging for Data:
Meta Data

When collected and maintained, meta data lays out the physical data structures in the target system including:

- The data elements and their data types
- The business definition for all of the data elements
- How often each data element gets updated and by what person or process

Meta data is collected (identified and relegated to a central repository), maintained (synchronized automatically with the changing data architecture), and deployed (provided to end-users via the optimum tools).

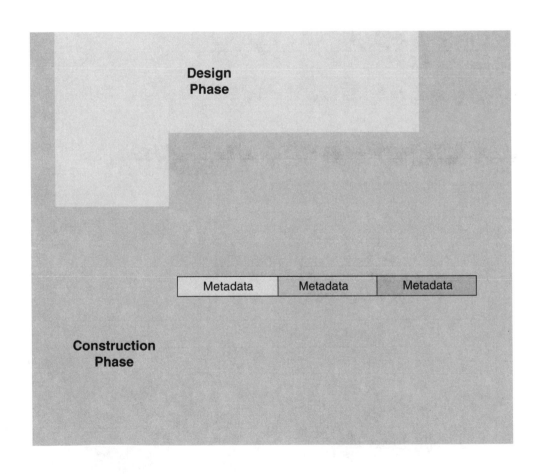

- Who in the company can be contacted for more information about each data element
- A list of the other data elements in other systems that have the same business meaning
- The valid values for each data element

Meta data is data about data. Got it?! Meta data enables the meta data administrator to: 1) find *what* data is in the warehouse; and 2) determine *how* to use that data more efficiently. Because the data warehouse serves the business rather than the technical community, the formal establishment and ongoing support of meta data becomes significant in the data warehouse environment.

Meta data plays a key role in providing the information for defining, building, managing, and maintaining the data warehouse. It comes from many different sources, such as database catalogs, data dictionaries, modeling tools, and program copybooks. Every operational data system you own has meta data of some kind. In data warehousing, all the meta data in your organization falls into two categories: technical meta data and business meta data.

Technical meta data describes data elements as they exist in the source legacy systems and data warehouse. It also includes specifications for how the data is extracted, filtered, transformed, cleansed, and aggregated. In addition, it provides the information that controls the schedules for the processes that accomplish those tasks. Technical meta data is used by the data warehouse administrators and software tools that drive the data warehouse. This meta data is used to define the data warehouse model. The model is typically defined by a number of "business views" that relate closely to how business users want to use the data. By structuring the data into business subject areas, creation of the business views becomes very meaningful to the users and makes the transition to their business applications easier. Integration of these products provides the capability to share meta data.

In contrast, business meta data is required by business users to understand exactly what is in the data warehouse, what it means, the level of currency, and so forth—in business terms that are easy for business users to understand. Most of the business meta data comes from the technical meta data. Some descriptive information may have to be added based on input from the business users. The business meta data describes data elements and other "information objects," such as tables, queries, charts, and reports. This type of meta data is important because it gives users access to much more information, in addition to simple data elements. This would include "business views" of the data that represent the data warehouse model.

To enable you to support the acquisition and use of meta data throughout the enterprise, this chapter discusses how to use meta data for mapping data, how to manage meta data, and how to navigate meta data. Your objective is to provide integrated and consistent meta data across all the different areas and uses with the data warehouse.

See Chapter 4 for a discussion of meta data tools. We recommend purchasing a tool to decrease the potential of human error resulting from manual coding, to shorten the time required to complete the task, and to generate task documentation automatically.

Using Meta Data for Mapping Data

Meta data is used for *mapping* data from the operational environment into the data warehouse (see Table 8–1). Attributes, conversions, changes in naming conventions, and changes in physical characteristics of data are examples of what the meta data administrator maps from the operational environment to the data warehouse. And, every time a data element from one source is mapped to the data warehouse, the meta data administrator documents the connection between the data elements, as well as any transformation that takes place.

Table 8–1 Source-to-Target Meta Data Mapping Table

POS_Load Table		
Data Warehouse <u>Target</u> Table Field Name	**Description**	**<u>Source</u> Host DBMS File/Table.Field Name**
store_number	Store number	**Mapped** from Mainframe; DB2 ITEM_SALES_TABLE.str_num
day_number	Business day number	**Mapped** from Mainframe; DB2 ITEM_SALES_TABLE.day_no
shift_number	Store shift number	**Mapped** from Mainframe; DB2 ITEM_SALES_TABLE.shift_no
transaction_uid	Internal sequence number for the transaction	**Mapped** from Mainframe; DB2 ITEM_SALES_TABLE.trans_uid
pos_sequence_number	Sequence number of the item in the transaction	**Mapped** from Mainframe; DB2 ITEM_SALES_TABLE.sequence_no
transaction_type_code	Transaction type code: 1 - Item sales 2 - Department sales	**Mapped** from Mainframe; DB2 ITEM_SALES_TABLE.transtyp

Table 8–1 Source-to-Target Meta Data Mapping Table *(continued)*

POS_Load Table		
sales_date	Date of sale	**Mapped** from Mainframe; DB2 TRANSACTION.end_date
sales_time	Time of sale in HHMMSS format using 24-hr clock	**Mapped** from Mainframe; DB2 TRANSACTION.end_time
upc	Universal product code	**Mapped** from Mainframe; DB2 ITEM_SALES_TABLE.plu_nbr
department_number	Department number	**NULL** for item sales
record_amount	Recorded sales amount	**Mapped** from Mainframe; DB2 ITEM_SALES_TABLE.record_amount
record_count	Number of units sold	**Mapped** from Mainframe; DB2 ITEM_SALES_TABLE.record_count
sales_unit	Sales number of units	**Derived** from record_count
sales_retail	Sales retail amount	**Derived** from record_amount
gross_profit	Gross profit from units sold	**Derived** as follows: Gross profit = sales_retail - sales_cost sales_cost can be derived by multiplying the sales_unit by unit_cost. unit_cost will be sourced from the PRODUCT Dimension table. And, for departments, it cannot be computed.
market_id	Market dimension key	**Found** from the MARKET Dimension table using store_number
time_id	Time dimension key	**Found** from the TIME Dimension table using sales_date
product_id	Product dimension key	**Found** from the PRODUCT Dimension table using upc or department number.
unit_cost	Unit cost for the product	unit_cost will be sourced from the PRODUCT Dimension table.
record_number	Number of records loaded in this run	System-generated

Meta Data Management

Meta data also enables the *management of data over time*. In the data warehouse, a time horizon of five to ten years is typical, while a time horizon of a few weeks to 90 days is normal for the operational environment. Because of the historical nature of the data, the structure of the data (keys, attributes, layouts)—or, the underlying table schema—also changes. To be effective, meta data management must:

- Provide a means of capturing and storing meta data in a time-variant manner
- Capture meta data from a variety of sources, including CASE, data acquisition and data access tools, as well as operational sources
- Integrate various technical and business meta data from sources meaningful to the end-user
- Enable end-users to navigate the meta data and understand the data from a business perspective

In addition, the meta data administrator identifies:

- Business definitions of the data (see Table 8–2)
- Technical definitions of the data
- Update/refresh dates
- Data flow diagrams
- Context diagrams
- Data quality indicators
- Data sources, such as corporate repositories, operational systems, documentation, CASE tools, extraction tools, and cleansing tools
- Strategies for obtaining and capturing the data from each source
- Programs, processes, and procedures for ongoing maintenance

Table 8–2 Business Meta Data Fact or Measure Definitions

Business Measure	Description
# of Stores Selling	The number of stores selling the selected PRODUCT for the selected MARKET during the selected TIME.
GP $	Estimated gross profit for POS sales. GP$ = (POS Unit Retail - PRODUCT SRP) * POS Units Sold
GP$ % Chg vs PY	Gross profit $ percent change versus prior year.

Table 8–2 Business Meta Data Fact or Measure Definitions *(continued)*

Business Measure	Description
GP%	Gross profit percent for the selected PRODUCT for the selected MARKETduring the selected TIME.
Net GP$	Estimated gross profit from POS sales, offset by any associated credits.
Net GP %	Net gross profit percent for POS sales, offset by any associated credits.
Sales $	Dollars sold for the selected PRODUCT for the selected MARKET during the selected TIME. Based on POS sales data.
Sales $ % Chg vs PY	Sales units percent change versus prior year.
Sales Units	Units sold for the selected PRODUCT for the selected MARKET during the selected TIME. Based on POS sales data.
Sales Units % Chg vs PY	Sales units percent change versus prior year.
SRP	Suggested retail price from the current PRODUCT Dimension table, updated from the host DB2 system. Evaluated independently of the selected TIME.

Due to its potentially lengthy shelf-life, meta data must be *versioned* (or, changes continuously tracked over time). Versioning can be accomplished by placing the effective *from* date and the effective *to* date on the meta data component; or, by placing the effective *from* date only on the meta data component and deriving the effective *to* date by looking at the next occurrence of the data component.

Elements tracked via the meta data include the following: extract history; alias information (attribute and key information that allows for alternative names); status information (number of rows currently in a table, growth rate, usage statistics, and indexing); relationship history; contact person the DSS analyst can call to understand the data; and, access patterns (use when determining what aggregates need to be built for performance and when data needs to be migrated to other media).

Navigating the Meta Data

End-users able to easily access meta data in an understandable form can learn:

- What entities are defined in the warehouse, as well as the business rules implemented for those entities
- What attributes are populated for the subject area of interest, and the definitions and values of those attributes
- What the sources of data are for each entity, including both applications systems and external data sources
- What data marts are available to enable easier access to subsets of the data
- What queries have already been written that access relevant subject areas

Because data warehouses hold data downloaded and filtered from various operational stores (and the data has probably changed over time), the meta data must instruct both technical and business users about how the data arrived in the warehouse, where it came from, and how it was transformed. The meta data must also be tightly linked to documentation that can assist implementors in the rapid deployment phase of the life cycle. Basically, users need to know what data is available and what the data means in clear, non-technical terms.

Collecting meta data is not the challenge for most organizations; rather, the challenge is integrating the various tools (for example, the extraction, administration, and query tools) that create and maintain their own meta data. Integration is promising to become less complex, particularly via the Metadata Coalition's meta data interchange specification, which proposes a file exchange definition. (Note, however, that the specification does not address model reconciliation, versioning control, and conflict resolution, nor is it a certification program provided to validate compliance.)

Integration of meta data into data access and analysis tools can be accomplished in several ways. One is side-by-side access to meta data and real data (meta data is displayed in one tool concurrently with data warehouse queries in another tool). Or, query tool help text can be populated with meta data exported from a central meta data store. Or, your organization can provide end-users with query tools that are *meta data*-aware. Optimally, inter-connectivity between the meta data tool and query tool is enabled.

To address the complexity created by huge data warehouses and multiple data marts, many vendors offer tools that eliminate steps during the complex transformation process. For example, it only takes a single step to merge multiple sequential files, integrate them, and then output the multiple files in a many-to-many manner. Moreover, these tools are able to mask or define the layout of date fields when moving data or business rules from sources to target databases.

Consider the following when reviewing meta data integration software:

- Integrity
- Process time/bottlenecks
- Version testing time
- Information model reconciliation
- Information model changes/conversions
- Infrastructure and process costs
- Utilization of central model control
- Integration with end-user access tool

Products focusing on meta data management, such as Prism Solution's Directory Manager and IBM's DataGuide, provide facilities to maintain synonyms for use by end-users. But, procedures and controls must be put in place to assure that changes to operational systems are properly reflected in these meta data directories.

Prism has also incorporated front-end access, enabling users to launch end-user access tools like those from Cognos Corp., Brio Technology Inc., Business Objects Inc., and MicroStrategy Inc. Leveraging the tool's ability to capture meta data, Prism Warehouse Executive allows administrators to annotate the meta data—the historical requirements that drove the creation of the meta data—and store it within the Prism Warehouse Directory.

As data warehouses scale, enterprises need an automated framework that helps administrators distribute and track changes. These dynamic architectures must respond to modifications to data warehouses and/or data marts, particularly in the number of data sources or in the combinations of data from those sources, in underlying warehouse technologies, and ultimately, in the informational content the warehouse or data marts provide to users.

The recursive nature of data warehouse development demands that meta data be accurate and current for it to be useful. You must create a physical information directory for storing the physical data model, which represents the meta data that is essential for a comprehensible, useable data warehouse environment. Assuming a meta data management tool is used, the physical design is usually predefined.

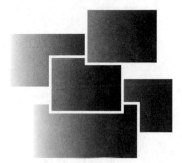

Chapter 9

SHOW ME THE DATA: END-USER ACCESS

The goal of the data warehouse is about to be achieved! You've staffed your project, selected your tools, implemented your design, and stocked data in the warehouse. The moment of truth is at hand—end-user access, data mining, and Internet accessibility are nearly feasible, nearly possible, nearly achievable....

A good end-to-end decision support solution must take into consideration the differing needs of the end-user community. The database administrator must

End-users are looking for previously unknown patterns in the data; relationships that have, so far, gone undiscovered. Use the wrong tool, and they will remain undiscovered.

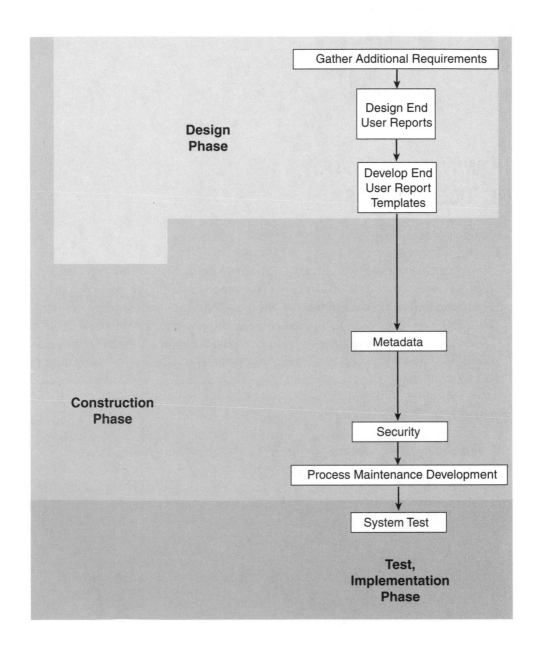

enable and support the tools necessary to support a broad range of users. They range from simple, easy-to-use query and report-writing capabilities to robust, enterprisewide decision support systems, which must be scaleable and integrated with a complete set of capabilities necessary to provide an end-to-end solution. No matter how well-designed, well-maintained, or intelligently configured a data warehouse is, it is useless without the right decision support tools for end-users. Users need to be able to display, analyze, and discover data. And, they need tools that meet their skill levels.

Some users simply need access to the information in a warehouse. They need to be able to select from a set of queries and reports, possibly modifying them slightly. For more sophisticated power users, particularly those interested in multidimensional analysis and data mining, more robust decision support capabilities are required. (Multidimensional analysis is the ability to look at a data set and analyze it from multiple perspectives, or dimensions, and run a query with multiple constraints.) Data mining is the ability to analyze patterns and relationships that result in answers to questions you might never have thought to ask. This chapter first discusses end-user tool architecture, then reviews data mining concepts and tools. We then take a look at how to leverage the Internet for data access.

End-user Tool Architecture

The selection of the right end-user tool is paramount to obtaining the best possible information from the warehouse, and hence, the best possible return on investment.

How do you identify the best end-user access tool for your organization? Users should be guided step-by-step through whatever forms of analysis (for example, forecasting, linear regression, and *What if?*) are required. (People shouldn't need to know SQL, or where data resides, and they shouldn't be able to generate queries which kill the network). End-user access tools should enable drill-down, drill-up, and drill-across, as well as specify conditions or criteria to apply to the data sources. The user should be notified when a change in the data means that previous assumptions and queries are no longer valid and must be re-run.

See Chapter 4 for a comparison of end-user access tools. We recommend purchasing a tool to shorten the time required to complete the task, to enable sophisticated data access, and to highlight previously unobserved patterns in the data.

End-user access tools first enabled ad hoc or unstructured access to corporate data, allowing power users in the information technology group to generate reports themselves. Then came more sophisticated query and reporting tools with a descriptive set of meta data to substitute more friendly business terms for the underlying table column names and table relations. Point-and-click automatic report generation capabilities were added next, making major advances in ease of use (see Figure 9–1).

Query Tool Architecture

Figure 9–1 Query tool architecture.

The need to do more sophisticated analysis beyond the limitations of SQL led to the development of OLAP tools, or multidimensional database (MDD) tools. MDDs go beyond the limitations of SQL, enabling analytical functionality in the server (see Figure 9–2).

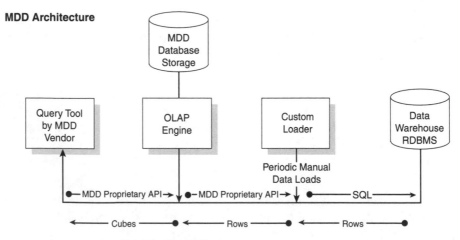

Figure 9–2 Multidimensional tool architecture.

MDD is a specialized engine that stores data in a proprietary array format that is commonly referred to as a **cube**. This cube corresponds to the business dimensions understood by users. Example business dimensions are: geography or location, product, customer, and time.

Relational OLAP (ROLAP) heralded the combination of relational and multidimensional architectures. A scaleable, parallel, relational database provides store capability and high-speed access to the underlying data. A middle analysis tier provides the multidimensional conceptual view of the data and the extended analytical functionality that is not available in SQL. The presentation tier delivers results to the users. These systems provide the benefits of fully analytical functionality while maintaining the openness, scalability, and performance of leading RDBMSs. The database design technique is known as *dimensional modeling* and is exemplified by the *star schema*. These tools also have a more robust set of meta data for hierarchies and drill paths which effectively insulates the end-users from the underlying relational model (see Figure 9–3).

Relational OLAP Architecture

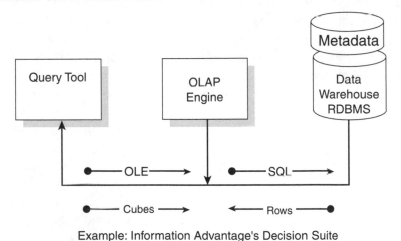

Example: Information Advantage's Decision Suite

Figure 9–3 ROLAP architecture.

Traditional query and reporting tools generally load all the raw data into the warehouse and let the query tool ask questions. The formulation of the query results is done at query execution time. Consequently, performance is unacceptable and results are less sophisticated than when using MDD or ROLAP. MDD pre-calculates the results of every query, enabling a fast response, but causing inordinate delays and scaleability problems when loading the system (in other words, a long batch window that won't scale above 50GB). ROLAP systems balance the storage/performance tradeoff by allowing either pre-calculation of data or calculation on-the-fly.

Additionally, ROLAP accommodates:

- Parallelization: Enables storage of massive amounts of data; breaks down complex actions into smaller parts, each of which can be executed in parallel
- Data Partitioning: Enables the database to automatically distribute portions of a table or tables in more than one piece, which enhances the ability of the database to parallelize operations and eases maintenance of large data sets; also enables the database to distribute data over multiple physical storage devices, improving the system's read/write performance
- Indexes: Supports star joins and bit-mapped indexes

Vendors are now moving to an integrated ROLAP model. In a traditional ROLAP system, the analysis engine formulates optimized SQL statements that are sent to the RDBMS server. The analysis engine then takes the data back from the server, re-integrates it, and performs further analysis and computations before delivering the finished results to the user. This usually means that data travels over the network twice: once to the analysis server, and again to the client application. The next logical step would be the integration of the ROLAP engine with the scaleable, parallel RDBMS, enabling integrated ROLAP. Integrated ROLAP would support internal parallelism, integrated optimizers, and parallel loading, thus enabling the loading of the detail data and derived summary-level data in a single pass, a parallel load step. Data mining software could also be integrated. Typically, the data mining software is physically separate from the database. But, leveraging the extensible database technology of the major DBMS vendors would enable mining technology to be embedded in the database. For example, Informix's DataBlade technology integrates the INFORMIX-MetaCube OLAP engine; the DB2 Universal Database Extenders technology integrates Arbor's Essbase.

The data warehouse is designed to provide a source of clean, reliable, accessible, well-defined, and well-documented data to the organization. Access to this data is enabled via:

- **Query and reporting**: Enables users to access enterprise data for reporting and graphing without having to know SQL; query tools enable users to answer questions in lists (For example, a user could ask (and expect an answer to) something similar to: "Retrieve all products costing between $50 and $125 purchased from ABC Supply Company on May 1, 1996.")
- **Multidimensional analysis**: OLAP (or multidimensional) tools empower the business user to look for causative factors exploring *Why?* and *What if?* versus the traditional *What?* (For example, one could ask: "Compared to the previous year, how have the last 12 months of increased advertising expenditures impacted my product sales in NYC compared to San Francisco?")
- **Data mining**: Provides organizations with the ability to analyze and monitor trends and variations within their businesses that provide information to aid the decision-making process
- **4GL-developed applications**: Provide screen painters with 4GLs to provide query, reporting, graphing, and multidimensional analysis without programming; but, they result in less flexible black-box information technology applications

When choosing an end-user access tool, consider what functionality is required. For example, do your end-users require basic reporting (no summaries or aggregations), variance reporting (estimates versus actual), technical analysis (calculations), complex reporting (summaries and aggregations), trend analysis (time series-based), multidimensional analysis, strategic analysis, data mining, and/or data visualization?

Data Mining

Data mining is the process of discovering meaningful new correlations, patterns, and trends by sifting through large amounts of data stored in repositories, using pattern recognition technologies and statistical and mathematical techniques.

> **Data mining** is the process of automatically extracting previously unknown and important predictive information from databases, and using it to make crucial business decisions.

The data warehouse provides one logical view of an organization's data which may bring together many distributed, heterogeneous data sources. Once the data warehouse is functional, the process of data mining can take place. Data mining enables organizations to analyze and monitor business trends and variations that provide information to aid the decision-making process.

Data mining is not specific to any industry. All that's required is a number of structured data sets and exploratory prowess. Enterprises in any industry sector—regardless of the precise nature of their data sets—can take advantage of intelligent technologies to tackle data mining. Infrastructure costs associated with a data mining project are highlighted in Figure 9–4. Organizations use data mining to reveal surprisingly significant facts, relationships, trends, patterns, exceptions, and anomalies, enabling them to:

- Visualize (data mining enables analysts to cleverly display huge amounts of data)
- Discover (data mining enables organizations to determine explicit hidden relationships, patterns, or correlations from data)
- Correct (when consolidating massive databases, many enterprises find that the data is not complete or contains errors)

Traditional database queries are designed to supply answers to simple questions, such as: "What were my sales in November 1996 in the Southwest region?" Multidimensional analysis lets users do much more complex queries, such as compare sales relative to plan by quarter and region for the prior two

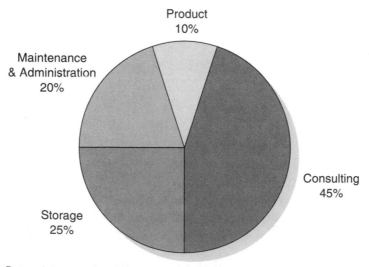

Figure 9–4 Data mining cost breakdown.

years. But in both cases, the results are merely extracted values or an aggregation of values. Data mining finds patterns in the data and infers rules from them. Those patterns and rules can be used to guide decision-making and forecast the effect of those decisions. And, data mining can speed analysis by focusing attention on the most important variables.

Data mining is taking off for several reasons. Organizations are gathering more data about their businesses. The enormous drop in storage prices has made it feasible to keep huge amounts of detailed data online. And, the dramatic drop in the cost/performance ratio of computers has enabled organizations to start applying the complex algorithms used in data mining.

Data Mining Tools

So, how does one find the tool to perform these miracles? Ask data mining tool vendors the following questions:

- *How many examples can be handled simultaneously?*
- *How much pre-processing is required?* (Complete tools should come with database access, translation, and pre-processing capabilities.)
- *Does the tool support both top-down and bottoms-up analysis?* (Users should be able to test hypotheses using specific facts or records (top-down analysis). The system should also support building hypotheses from individual facts while allowing users to modify the facts to perform *What if?* investigations (bottoms-up).
- *Does the system output rules, models, decision trees, or numbers?* (If an explanation of the results is paramount, rules and induction techniques are appropriate. If finding the best combination of factors is the goal, use neural networks and fractal techniques.)
- *How easily can a model be updated when new information is available?*
- *How much effort and expertise are required to use the technology?*

Data mining falls into five categories, including associations, sequences, classifications, clusters, and forecasting.

- In *sequences,* events are linked over time
- *Classification* helps discover, for example, customer characteristics and provides a model to predict who these customers are
- *Clustering* is similar to classification, but differs in that no groups have yet been defined
- *Forecasting* estimates the future value of continuous variables (like sales figures) based on patterns within the data

The main types of data mining tools are neural networks, decision trees, rule induction, and data visualization. *Data visualization* relies on human analysis. But, even the best set of rules or tables of data may reveal more information when visualized with color in two-dimensional (2-D), 3-D, or 4-D (3-D with animation) representations. *Rule induction* is the process of reasoning from specific facts to reach a hypothesis. *(Facts* in data mining applications refer to database records, and *hypothesis* refers to a decision tree that attempts to divide data in a meaningful way.) Parameters used to control induction routines include rule length, the maximum or minimum number of rules to generate, a measure of rule confidence, a margin for error, and a minimum portion of the database that must be scanned for the rule to be considered valid. *Neural networks* are multi-layered network architectures that "learn" how to solve a problem based on examples. Note that neural networks require extensive data pre-processing. *Decision trees* divide the data into groups based on variable values resulting in a hierarchy of *if-then* statements that classify the data. Some decision trees have problems handling continuous sets of data, like age or sales, and require that the data be grouped into ranges (see Figure 9–5).

Rule-Based Data Mining via Decision Trees

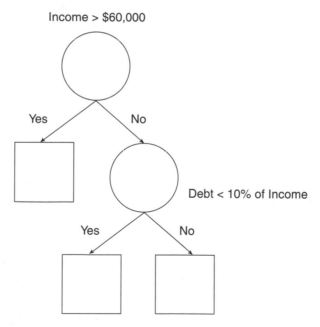

Figure 9–5 Rule-based data mining via decision trees.

Leveraging the Internet

The Internet offers a solution to the delivery of data warehouse information to end-users throughout the enterprise and around the world. With the right tools and the right architecture, the data warehouse can be made accessible over the enterprise intranet, forming the basis for an enterprise information infrastructure. When the data warehouse is put on the intranet, users can toggle between structured data analysis (producing reports in columns and rows) and unstructured browsing.

At a high level, the goal of data warehousing and the goal of the Web are the same: easy access to data. The value of a data warehouse is maximized when the right data is in the hands of those who need it, regardless of when and where they need it. However, corporations have typically had to struggle with complex client/server architectures to give end-users the access they need. Mix in the additional issues that arise when you try to give remote users access to the warehouse, and the result is often a truly complex environment. In addition, all users need training on how to use client applications. The Web removes these issues because many of the same applications will work over the Internet, removing the complexity previously associated with supporting remote access. And, the client application is the same Web browser that is used for every other Web application, meaning that most users are already familiar with it.

There are many technical issues that must be resolved prior to implementing Web access to the data warehouse. Reports created from data stored in the warehouse should not simply be shared as text files. All reports should include the underlying logic, giving the recipient the ability to immediately analyze and modify a report, as well as the logic and assumptions supporting the analyses. For effective collaboration, reports must be shared throughout the workgroup and enterprise. If recipients are not authorized, access to report logic should be denied. Agents must have the ability to run continually as background processes on an intranet server because each user is almost always disconnected from the Web server. Because data warehouses tend to grow exponentially, it is critical that agents proactively monitor and manage activities, alerting decision-makers when specific conditions exist.

A Web application needs either to maintain session information or to pass state information back and forth to the user via embedded HTML information. Either way, a unique session identifier is usually generated on the server end. What information a Web database application maintains and how smoothly it makes it available to the database developer are big considerations in choosing a development system. Also, the application server should be able to handle a large number of simultaneous connections. The more sophisticated products use a distributed processing architecture that can route application requests among multiple physical machines (for example, IBM's Network Dispatcher); most, however, simply rely on the Web server to limit the number of simultaneous connections. Another consideration is the number of simultaneous database connections required; the less required by the database product, the better.

The Common Gateway Interface (CGI) facility provides a method to execute server-resident software. However, most Internet applications provide all users with the same access permissions rather than mapping users to their server account by verifying user names and passwords. Also, the CGI interface does not offer a continuous connection to the database. As a result, it is impossible to support an application requiring multiple interactive queries—a data warehousing requirement. Perhaps the most significant challenge facing developers is the stateless nature of the Web. A Web server responds to page requests either by returning an HTML page or by triggering an external application via a server API. Once the page is delivered or the application executes, the transaction is complete and the connection closes. The server makes no provision for storing vital information about the application and the user within the application. This approach is fine for delivering hypertext documents, but creates huge headaches for anyone trying to design a tight, multi-page database application.

OLAP vendors are quickly providing new Web development tools that allow Web browsers access to data warehouses, including Arbor Software's Essbase Web Gateway, MicroStrategy's DSSWeb, and Information Advantage's WebOLAP. NetDynamics 2.0 from Spider Technologies generates applications as server-side Java code, and the NetDynamics application server handles data access, load balancing, and state information management. The environment provides security, from managing application flow to setting database privileges. The NetDynamics Studio is a productive GUI development environment whose wizards help build pages and SQL queries easily.

NeXT's WebObjects Enterprise 2.0, based on NeXT's object-oriented framework, offers a collection of tools for developing enterprise-level Web database applications. Its Enterprise Objects Modeler provides full application and data modeling capabilities, while the Enterprise Objects Framework offers the ability to abstract business logic from the database back-end and application interface. WebObjects also addresses the important areas of state management and transaction processing.

One tool being developed by a DBMS vendor is IBM's DB2 World Wide Web Connection Version 1 (WWWv1). WWWv1 is an Internet gateway tool which allows users to build Internet and intranet applications to access data in the enterprise. WWWv1 works as an Internet gateway to DB2 and other sources via IBM's DataJoiner middleware. WWWv1 supports INSERT, DELETE, SELECT, and UPDATE on DB2 data, and enables Internet application development with HTML and SQL. WWWv1 also supports data linking between queries. Additionally, it supports DB2 large objects, as well as authenticated access to DB2. A CGI run-time engine processes input from HTML forms and sends SQL commands to a DB2 system specified in the WWWv1 application. This application consists of a macro file containing HTML input and report form definitions, SQL commands, and variable definitions. The application user on the Web sees only a familiar Web page form that may prompt for user input and then kick off the application transaction, returning the DB2 query results in a familiar-looking Web page report. WWWv1 applications can take advantage of data linking, the capability to use data returned by an SQL query as input to one or more SQL commands that can drill down further into DB2 data. Authentication mechanisms include support of a user login and password authentication, which can be used to restrict user access. Or, the Internet server on which WWWv1 resides can be configured to protect certain directories on the DB2 server. Figure 9–6 illustrates how WWWv1 works.

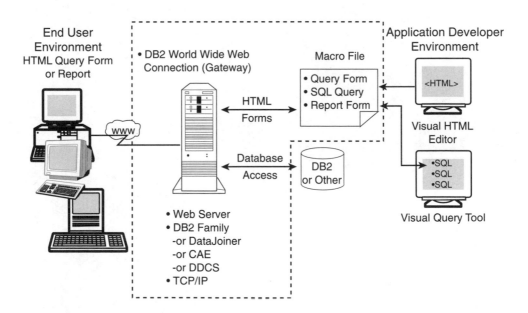

Figure 9–6 IBM's DB2 World Wide Web Connection Version 1. *Copied with permission from IBM.*

IBM's Net.Data, the follow-on to WWWv1, provides native access to DB2 on all platforms, as well as Oracle, Sybase, and file data. Net.Data supports the building of interactive Web sites with data from multiple sources, including relational data, flat file data, and Lotus Notes data. Net.Data optimizes access to advanced objects in the DB2 family, such as DB2 Relational Extenders and DB2 stored procedures. By integrating with specific Web server interfaces, Net.Data can operate as an extension of the Web server, delivering improved performance over CGI applications. Net.Data's application development environment includes a rich macro language, conditional logic, HTML and VRML support, HTML variable substitution, JDBC interface to DB2 data, and support for multiple data. You can imbed dynamic SQL, Java applets and JavaScripts, Perl, and REXX in your Net.Data application, or call DLLs written in C/C++.

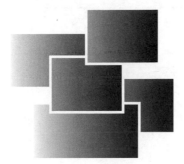

Chapter 10

UNDER CONSTRUCTION: CONSTRUCTION, TESTING AND ROLLOUT

The data warehouse construction incorporates the installation, configuration, and testing of the server, technical workstations, end-user access workstations, communications services, DBMS, system software, scheduler application, performance monitoring and tuning tools, end-user application software, and meta data. It also includes the designing, building, debugging, and testing of each

Construction is the physical act of implementing the designed data warehouse environment.

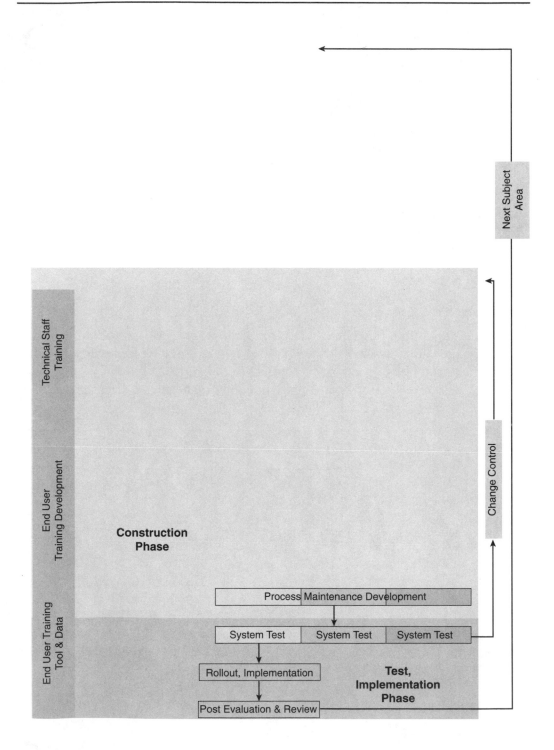

extraction, transformation, and scrubbing application. The testing scenario requires fully testing the links between the operational environment and the data warehouse, ensuring that the DASD and CPU are sufficient.

The best advice we can offer with the data warehouse construction is to plan, schedule, and ask for assistance from your product vendors with the integration of each piece. Approach the construction, rollout, and testing phases of the data warehouse deployment as the implementation of the team's plans, as the continuous measurement of work-in-progress, and as a feedback tool to resolve problems and improve performance. This approach will provide visibility into the process, and effective control of both the process and its resultant products. You can use this checklist as a project management entry tool to identify all elements of the project to be controlled and identify intermediate elements produced by the development process.

(Note that following and adhering to this checklist can provide visibility and control into the management process, ensuring that cost, schedule, and technical performance meet each project objective. A precise set of reviews and reports can be established to monitor task completion. Tools—such as the Microsoft Project application and project file reviewed in Chapter 3—can be used to track critical path schedules and resource expenditures. This approach will control the project profile baselines. In addition, you will have the ability to identify, account for, monitor, and control any element that the project is dependent upon and is outside the project's span of control.)

Construction, Testing and Rollout Checklist

Use the following checklist as a tool to both understand and control your data warehouse deployment.

Install, Configure, and Test

Development Environment

	YES	NO	NA
Data Extraction (Programmer's Workstation)	☐	☐	☐
Report Tool Software (Developer's Workstation)	☐	☐	☐
Compilers, Debuggers, and Tools	☐	☐	☐

	YES	NO	NA
Server Environment			
Processing Environment (HW, OS, DASD, and Scheduler)	☐	☐	☐
DBMS	☐	☐	☐
End-user Access Engine	☐	☐	☐
Performance and Monitoring Tools	☐	☐	☐
Meta Data Software Installed and Repository Configured	☐	☐	☐
Network Inter-connectivity (Gateway, Switches, Adapters, and Cables)	☐	☐	☐

Construct/Create

	YES	NO	NA
Database Objects (Tablespace Files, Tables, Indexes, Users, and Grants)	☐	☐	☐
Atomic-level Data Extraction/Acquisition Programs	☐	☐	☐
Atomic-level Data Load Programs	☐	☐	☐
Atomic-level Data Scrubbing/ Transformation Programs	☐	☐	☐
Atomic-level Post-load Program to Summarize to Desired Grain	☐	☐	☐
Departmental-level Aquisition/Load Programs	☐	☐	☐
Departmental-level Post-load Programs	☐	☐	☐
Predefined End-user Access Application Programs	☐	☐	☐
Predefined Facts/Measures and Templates for Ad Hoc Access	☐	☐	☐
Load Technical and Business Meta Data	☐	☐	☐
History Data Load	☐	☐	☐

Schedule and Validate

	YES	NO	NA
Referential Integrity, Unique Indexes, and Check Constraints	☐	☐	☐
Test Scenarios	☐	☐	☐
Schedule Batch Extractions, Transformations, and Load Batch Programs	☐	☐	☐
Backup DBMS	☐	☐	☐
DBMS Statistics for Optimizer	☐	☐	☐
Data Load	☐	☐	☐
Post-atomic Process	☐	☐	☐
Departmental Process	☐	☐	☐
Post-departmental Process	☐	☐	☐
Predefined Canned Reports	☐	☐	☐
Schedule Distribution of Canned Reports	☐	☐	☐
Security Is Read-only at: Database, Table, Row, Column, Front-end Access Tool, Network, and Operating System Levels	☐	☐	☐
Monitoring Applications	☐	☐	☐

Does data reorganization need to be performed?
Is an index poorly structured?
How much data is in overflow?
What is the statistical composition of the data?
What data is accessed and how frequently?
Who is accessing the data?
What detailed data is summarized repeatedly?

Define Processes and Procedures

	YES	NO	NA
Monitoring Usage and Ongoing Performance	☐	☐	☐
Security	☐	☐	☐
Meta Data Versioning, Updating, and Management	☐	☐	☐
Batch Load Error Correction Procedures	☐	☐	☐
Archive/Restore	☐	☐	☐
Operational Manuals (Batch Operators, DBAs)	☐	☐	☐
End-user Access Training Database/Sample Data	☐	☐	☐
End-user Access Training Documentation	☐	☐	☐

End-user Access Training Documentation
(Include known error messages (network connection down, database down, limitations of access tool), tips on performing drilling, selecting, scheduling, emailing, and collaboration, and data steward to contact for each subject area.)

	YES	NO	NA
Load History information	☐	☐	☐

Test

	YES	NO	NA
Unit Load and Post-load Programs	☐	☐	☐
Validate Test Scenarios	☐	☐	☐
Integration	☐	☐	☐
Cycle Tests of Process (OLTP->DW->End-user Workstation)	☐	☐	☐
Stress Testing/Volume Testing	☐	☐	☐
Verify Integration with Front-end Access Tools	☐	☐	☐

Data Quality

If possible, make any data changes to the source application. In reality, most databases will have to cleanse the data prior to loading the data warehouse. Proactively log all warning messages on problem data as you load it, and route the log to the data steward responsible for data quality. Consider loading the data rather than just putting it into an exception log file, making issues visible to the business analysts and managers looking at the data. Analysts and managers can then put pressure on the re-engineering process (as many organizations are now using the data warehouse as a re-engineering driver).

Documentation (Process Maintenance Development)

The following documentation should to be added to the existing analysis and design documents—the scope, assumptions, source systems, logical and physical data models, meta data, end-user access requirements, and programming (extraction, transformation, and loading documents—created in Chapters 3 through 9).

1. End-user Training Document

   - General overview of the data warehouse and expected value that will result
   - Definition of the data in the warehouse
   - Instructions for navigating the meta data
   - Instructions for using the data access application
   - Instructions for adding users and/or data
   - Help desk phone numbers, and data steward's name and number

2. Operations Document

   - Help desk schedule and responsibilities
   - Batch job schedule
   - Application components and cost of downtime
   - Service agreements
   - Hardware configuration
   - Database configuration
   - Backup and recovery procedures

Change Control

To ensure proper program development standards, use some form of change control mechanism, for example, a Source Code Control System *(gets* and *puts).* After establishing the initial project scope, any potential scope changes should go through a formal review process. A sample change request form follows (see Table 10–1).

Table 10–1 Sample change control request form

CHANGE CONTROL REQUEST FORM
REQUESTER
REQUESTER NAME   TELEPHONE #
MACHINE #   DATE REQUESTED
TIME REQUESTED   DURATION OF CHANGE
DESCRIPTION
DESCRIPTION (Enter a brief description of the change)
JUSTIFICATION (Why is this change required? What benefits will result?
TECHNICAL IMPACT DOES THIS CHANGE REQUIRE A PRE-IMPLEMENTATION TEST PLAN? DEFINE:
DOES THIS CHANGE REQUIRE A POST-IMPLEMENTATION TEST PLAN? DEFINE:
RISK ASSESSMENT WHAT IS THE CUSTOMER OR ENVIRONMENT RISK IF THIS CHANGE IS PERFORMED?
WHAT IS THE CUSTOMER OR ENVIRONMENT RISK IF THIS CHANGE DOESN'T WORK?

Testing

Ensuring that the data warehouse environment has achieved integration success requires *testing* the:

- Atomic data acquisition process
- Atomic-level load
- Atomic-level post-load summarizations, as well as the departmental load transformation process, including the extraction, summarization, derivations, transport, and loading
- Maintenance processing
- Data administration tasks, including security, archiving, restoring, data acquisition and access, and data validation
- Data warehouse performance after loading huge volumes of data and enabling large groups of concurrent users

When the data warehouse is populated and your update procedures have been implemented, put the data warehouse into production rather than undertaking rigorous end-user testing. Why? End-users have already significantly participated in the data warehouse design; and, it's pretty difficult to simulate production volume and the number of users simultaneously accessing the data in a test environment. Consider accumulating volumes of actual data in a production setting to effectively test the data access methods.

> **Regression** testing ensures that any corrections or alterations made to the data warehouse components during testing activities do not affect the components not altered.

When testing, your primary focus should be on ensuring the ability of the technical environment to support the entire extract, transformation, and load processes. In addition, end-user access to the data is verified and assessed in terms of capabilities and performance. Based on the atomic data acquisition, atomic-level load, post-load, secondary departmental load/transformation, and maintenance procedures, complete a full cycle to execute the program code, scripts, and jobs for the current implementation. The main objective is to ensure that all the programs and processes execute and function as designed with an expanded set of data. Remember to:

- Confirm the accuracy of your test results
- Test end-user response time

- Involve end-users in evaluating results
- Modify data access methods as required by evaluating the results

Rollout and Training

The *rollout* process revolves around end-user acceptance. Training sessions are held and the production data warehouse is made available to a limited group of end-users (approximately five). The test plan is executed, allowing data access in a controlled environment. Ask your end-users to make recommendations concerning training materials and/or the overall capabilities of the data warehouse, identifying problems that can be quickly addressed with minimal impact. Consider obtaining approval in writing from your executive sponsor prior to general release of the data warehouse. As you get closer to releasing your DSS for production, plan your software and/or application distribution. Ideally, your software should be installed via the network rather than one desktop at a time.

After making the data warehouse generally available, use automated tools to monitor:

- Data access: Ensure that performance is adequate and data quality problems are identified and resolved
- Data loading: Ensure that the time required to load the data into the data warehouse falls within estimates
- CPU utilization
- DASD management

Initially, interest in the data warehouse will be high, with many end-users frequently accessing the data. It is important to monitor data access and performance patterns over time to identify normal utilization patterns. Development of detailed usage logs, reported problems, and system performance can contribute to the monitoring, analysis, and optimization of the data warehouse environment.

Remember that most users have no idea of the functionality that sophisticated decision support tools can offer. Because of this, design ongoing end-user training programs. Training should focus on:

- An introduction to data warehouse concepts
- An introduction to each person's data and how it relates to reports with which they are familiar
- Tool mechanics
- The types of analysis that can be performed

Finally, develop a support structure. The first and most obvious method of support is to create and expand the help desk. This gives the client one place to call. The people at your help desk need to be skilled enough to work their way through a technical problem, but they also need to have an understanding of the business, the data that is in the warehouse, and how it can and should be used.

Post-implementation Review

Conduct a review session to assess the overall project impact and/or results, as well as to assess how satisfied the end-users are with the project's deployment. The review session should:

- Document the overall development process and any recommended changes or adaptations to the methodology for future implementations.
- Review the testing process and results to determine any required changes and possible improvements
- Analyze the training material and its effectiveness in equipping end-users with the appropriate information
- Scrutinize your original sizing estimates and determine their degree of accuracy

Based on the findings of the post-implementation review, the data warehouse project manager should put together a document assessing the deployment, as well as recommending any changes. Note that the data warehouse is successful if the resulting implementation satisfies the original requirements and the end-users are satisfied. It's not successful if expectations weren't met (for example, the project scope was too broad and therefore unachievable, or a lack of communication occurred).

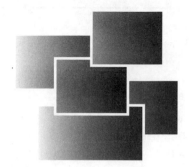

Chapter 11

IN CONCLUSION

Data warehousing is key for businesses wanting to turn their organizational data into an informational asset. Data warehousing is the basis for the analytical decision-making techniques that are critical in today's competitive environment. Data warehouses, exploited by such techniques as data mining and multi-dimensional data analysis and coupled with powerful parallel processing, can enhance the speed and accuracy at which customer's questions are formulated and answers are derived. What will decision makers consider the top drivers for data warehouse investments? Forrester Research, in "Data Warehouse Strategies," Volume 8, Number 6, September 1997, found that "42 percent of responses pointed to needing better data to guide decisions, while another 42 percent cited the drive for quicker issue resolution."

In this book, we've focused on the steps required to enable ease of use and broad access to data while advocating the advantages of implementing scalable hardware—we've identified the steps required to build a better warehouse while comparing and contrasting the best tools to:

- Access a variety of data sources for populating your data warehouse
- Transform the data into information using tools for cleansing, summarizing, and aggregating source data before placing it in the data warehouse
- Distribute the information to the locations where it makes the most sense for satisfying users' needs and makes the best use of your processing and storage resources

- Store all your data, including multidimensional and multimedia objects, on industrial-strength database management systems
- Manage and automate the data warehouse processes to maintain control and minimize the operational resource requirements
- Find and understand the information in the data warehouse and understand exactly what the warehouse information means in business terms
- Display, analyze, and discover the information and use it for business decision making

In the process of building your data warehouse, what trends should affect your decisions? A global economy is fostering the need to enable new ways of doing business. For example, a large retailer engages in inter-enterprise data access. Their inventory and point-of-sale data need to be open to suppliers to optimize deliveries. What about the continued move to networked client/server environments? Availability of adequate price/performance, capacity, and communication allows computing to be done on the end-user's desktop system. As the organization of a businesses is decentralized, expect data to be kept on distributed servers and decision makers to use personal-data-server products on their desktops.

Based on the Data Warehousing Institute's January 1996 User Survey, data warehouse project managers should plan for the number of users to double within the first six months and triple again with 24 months. Let your funding source know up front that you'll need money in six months and again in 18 months to handle increased processing demands and storage for hundreds of gigabytes and multi-terabytes of data. And, data warehouses are becoming more mission critical in that they are being relied on for tactical as well as strategic decisions requiring frequent updates and backup and restore procedures similar to mission-critical OLTP systems.

DBMS vendors will support a richer set of data types and will support compatibility for user-defined data-type extensions. Data-type extensions will include data structures and methods to operate on those new data types. Relational databases will have richer support for structured data as SQL is enhanced with object-oriented extensions. Object-oriented databases will see more set-oriented query extensions to complement support for user-defined data structures. To support richer function and data types, the optimization of database requests will become more sophisticated, becoming a performance differentiator. Trends in the distributed database area include data replication, two-phase commits, distributed queries, heterogeneous data access and join capability. By the end of the century, both OLTP and data warehouses will co-exist using the same databases. Database volumes will run in to the tens of terabytes. Data megastores will make data available as and when it happens increasing the value of information for purchase, for example, customer information lists.

On the other hand, some things will stay the same. Cost, performance and third-party application availability will continue to dictate database choice. The need for data consolidation, which in turn will shrink the number of databases Information Technology is required to support, will continue as companies move from mainframe systems to Oracle or DB2 on server platforms. Data administrators will continue to take an active role to help plan extracts and to work with the business administrator to define the data needs as well as gathering the information about the operational data and assisting in designing the data model that will be used for the DBMS.

Finally, expect data warehousing to become more significant in the discussions of knowledge management. Gartner Group Research (Foundations for Enterprise Knowledge Management, Business Process Re-engineering Strategic Analysis Report, April 7, 1997) defines knowledge management (KM) as an "emerging set of processes, organizational structures, applications, and technologies that aim to leverage the ability of the capable, responsible, autonomous individual to act quickly and effectively. KM achieves this end by providing this capable, responsible, autonomous individual with ready access to the enterprise's entire store of knowledge, including much of what is known but not documented. KM requires an integrated approach to identifying, managing, and—most importantly—sharing the enterprise's information assets, including databases, documents, policies, and procedures (e.g., 'explicit' knowledge) as well as undocumented expertise resident in individual workers (e.g., 'tacit' knowledge)."

Data warehousing via groupware and information retrieval technologies will be expected to support and manage the vast stores of information inundating enterprises. Active management of an enterprise's knowledge using the data warehouse will ensure that business practices are consistent, effective, and representative of the enterprise. Knowledge management serves as that final phase in the data warehousing process—the identification of knowledge as a critical resource and the arming of a company's personnel with this information. Because knowledge management requires integrated, on-line access to distributed information, data warehouse administrators and support staff will find themselves increasingly critical to coordinating the huge amounts of data coming online from uncoordinated projects.

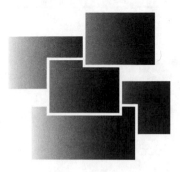

Terms and Technologies

Analytical Processing

Using the computer to produce an analysis for management decision, usually involving trend analysis, drill-down analysis, demographic analysis, and profiling. The data is often read-only and historical in nature.

Atomic

The lowest level of data granularity.

Bit-map Index

A specialized form on an index, indicating the existence or nonexistence of a condition for a group of records. Bit-maps are expensive to build and maintain, but provide very fast comparison and access facilities and take up less storage space than normal key indexes.

Database Key

A unique value that exists for each record in a database. The value is often indexed.

Data-driven Development

The approach to development that centers around identifying the commonality of data through a data model and building programs that have a broader scope than the immediate application.

DIS (Data Item Set)

A grouping of data items, each of which directly relates to the key of the grouping of data in which the data items reside. The data item set is part of the mid-level data model.

Data Mart

A subset of highly summarized data from the data warehouse designed to support the specific requirements of an organization.

Data Model

The logical data structures, including operations and constraints provided by DBMS for effective database processing. The system used for the representation of data (the ERD, or relational model).

Data Structure

A logical relationship among data elements that is designed to support specific data manipulation functions (trees, lists, and tables).

Data Warehouse

A collection of integrated, subject-oriented databases designed to support the DSS function, where each unit of data is relevant to some moment in time. The data warehouse contains atomic data and lightly summarized data.

DSS (Decision Support System)

A system used to support managerial decisions. A DSS analyzes many units of data in a heuristic fashion, but does not update the data. A DSS enables the process of using data to make both tactical and strategic decisions within an organization. Components of a DSS include ad hoc queries, reporting via reports, graphs, and charts, and analysis via slice, drill, and mine. Query, reporting, and analysis are interactive, enabling collaboration on each step.

Denormalization

To place normalized data in a duplicate location, thus optimizing the performance of the system.

Design Review

To review all aspects of a system prior to its physical implementation.

Drill-down Analysis

The type of analysis where examination of a summary number leads to the exploration of the components of the sum.

Data Transformation

Processing that changes the characteristics of data extracted from the operational system; integrates dissimilar data types; changes code; and selectively calculates, summarizes, and reconciles disparate update cycles.

Executive Information System (EIS)

GUI systems designed for top executives, featuring drill-down and trend analyses.

Extract

The process of selecting data from one environment and transporting it to another environment. See Data Transformation.

Granularity

The level of detail contained in a unit of data. The more detail there is, the lower the level of granularity; the less detail there is, the higher the level of granularity.

Hierarchies

Describe organizational structures and logical parent-child relationships within the data. An example would be in the market dimensions — *store -> market -> district -> region -> total country -> total global corporation.*

Heuristic

The mode of analysis in which the next step is determined by the results of the current step of analysis. Used for decision support processing.

Index

The portion of a storage structure maintained to provide efficient access to a record when its index key item is known.

Integrity

The property of a database that ensures that the data contained in the database is as accurate and consistent as possible.

JAD (Joint Application Design)

A group (usually end-users, together with the information technology group) that creates and refines application system requirements.

Meta Data

Data about data. Technical meta data reflects the description of the structure, content, keys, and indexes of data and their source of origin. Business meta data reflects definitions about measures (facts) used in calculations.

OLAP (Online Analytical Processing)

The OLAP Council defines online analytical processing as, "A category of software technology that enables analysis, managers and executives to gain insight into data through fast, consistent, interactive access to a wide variety of possible views of information that have been transformed from raw data to reflect the real dimensionality of the enterprise as understood by the user."

Operational Processing

Systems that run the day-to-day business for companies.

Partition

A segmentation technique in which data are divided into physically different units. Partitioning can be done at the application or system level.

Query Language

A language that enables an end-user to interact directly with a DBMS to retrieve and possibly modify data held under the DBMS.

Referential Integrity

The facility of a DBMS that ensures the validity of predefined relationships.

Rolling Summary

A form of storing archival data where the most recent data has the most details stored, and data that is older has fewer details stored.

Scope

The formal definition of what the boundaries of the system being modeled and/or developed are and are not.

SDLC (System Development Life Cycle)

The classical operational system development life cycle that typically includes requirements gathering, analysis, design, programming, testing, integration, and implementation.

System of Record

The definitive and singular source of operational data. If data element *abc* has a value of 25 in one database record and a value of 45 in the system of record, by definition, the first value is incorrect and must be reconciled. The system of record is useful for managing data redundancy.

Time-variant Data

Data whose accuracy is relevant to some moment in time. The three forms of time-variant data are: continuous timespan, event discrete, and periodic discrete.

Trend Analysis

The process of looking at homogeneous data over a spectrum of time.

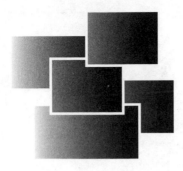

Acronyms

24x7	24-hours-a-day, seven-days-a-week
24x365	24-hours-a-day, 365-days-a-year
API	Application Programming Interface
BI	Business Intelligence
BPR	Business Process Re-engineering
CLI	Call Level Interface
DB	Database
DBA	Database Administrator
DDL	Data Definition Language
DLM	Distributed Lock Manager
DMPP	Distributed Memory Parallel Processing
DBMS	Database Management System
DSA	Dynamic Scaleable Architecture
DSS	Decision Support System
ERD	Entity Relationship Diagram
IS	Information System
I/O	Input/Output
MDD	Multidimensional Database
MDDBMS	Multidimensional Database Management System
MPP	Massively Parallel Processing
ODBC	Open Database Connectivity
ODS	Operational Data Store
OLAP	Online Analytical Processing
OLTP	Online Transaction Processing

OS	Operating System
PDQ	Parallel Data Query
RAID	Redundant Array of Independent Disks
RDBMS	Relational DBMS
RFI	Request For Information
ROI	Return On Investment
ROLAP	Relational Online Analytical Processing
SMP	Symmetric Multiprocessing
SMPP	Shared Memory Parallel Processing
SQL	Structured Query Language
TPS	Transactions Per Second
UDF	User-defined Functions
UDT	User-defined Types
VAX	Virtual Address Extension
VSD	Virtual Shared Disk

INDEX